Cambridge Marketing Handbook:
Distribution

Cambridge Marketing Handbook: Distribution

Models of Business Processes and Practice
A Marketing Perspective

Karl Meyer

Publisher's note

First published in Great Britain and the United States in 2013 by Kogan Page Limited in association with Cambridge Marketing Press.

120 Pentonville Road
London N1 9JN
United Kingdom

1518 Walnut Street, Suite 1100
Philadelphia PA 19102
USA

4737/23 Ansari Road
Daryaganj, New India
Delhi 110002

www.koganpage.com

© 2013 Cambridge Marketing College.

ISBN   978 0 7494 7065 4

British Library Cataloguing-in-Publication Data

A CIP record for this book is available from the British Library.

Design and layout by Cambridge Marketing College
Printed and bound by CPI/Antony Rowe, Chippenham, Wiltshire.

Dedication

To my wife, Paula, without whose determination to keep me at my desk this book would never have appeared. And my daughter, whose endless amazement that anybody would ever want to hear what I have to say keeps me grounded.

Biography

Karl has spent the past 20 years working within the internet industry in both technical and sales and marketing roles and was Director of Channel Marketing Strategy for WorldCom in EMEA. His roles took him across most of Europe and the Middle East, culminating in working for King Hussain of Jordan.

At present, Karl is working as the Product Marketing Manager for Dante Ltd. Dante provides leading edge networking solutions to the Research and Education community across Europe. This role acts as the interface between the end users and the development and support teams providing both the communications interface and the user advocate within the development of the next generation of networking technologies.

In addition Karl is an Associate at SPICE.co.uk – an online marketing agency focusing on delivering SEO, PPC, email marketing and social media marketing to deliver business growth to a wide variety of clients in the UK and overseas. His particular expertise is the use of web analysis and social media to target customers. Karl has an MBA from The Open University with a particular emphasis on International Enterprise Development and Knowledge Management and is a tutor at Cambridge Marketing College, teaching the Digital Programme.

Marketing is a continually evolving field and Karl is always keen to receive feedback and share the latest trends and thinking. He can be contacted at karl@spice.co.uk.

Contents

Wordle
Infographic
Acknowledgements
Introduction

Word cloud produced through Wordle™ (www.wordle.net)

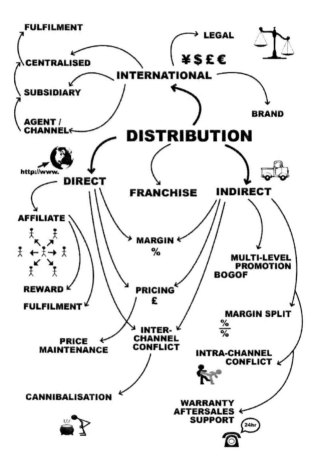

Infographic drawn by Lorna Brocklesby

Acknowledgements

It is often said that the best way to really understand a subject is to try to teach it. The breaking down of the whole into digestible pieces and re-assembly gives the tutor an immense insight into the subject matter. Therefore I am immensely grateful to Cambridge Marketing College for the opportunity to tutor and for the chance to write this small contribution to the understanding of the marketing process.

I am also grateful to WorldCom Ltd. who believed that an Internet engineer would turn out to be a passable Marketing and Business Consultant and to the tireless efforts of the Open University Business School for providing an academic grounding to complement the randomness of practical experience.

Introduction

Mention the word 'distribution' and the majority of people will immediately think of large warehouses full of pallets and fork-lift trucks and Eddie Stobart lorries rushing up and down the motorway network taking goods to shops across the country, wondering what exactly it has to do with marketing (excepting selling lots of toy lorries and giving them all cutesy names). Marketing and physical distribution just do not seem to mix.

It is true that distribution can involve lots of this type of lifting, shifting and shipping but that is far from the whole story and, within any business of any size, distribution consists of many business and marketing decisions. More comprehensively, it involves the understanding of how to place your business' products and services into the market, who will be involved in this placement and how this network of people and processes are interlinked and managed.

Many of these market management decisions and processes are considered to be unglamorous. Distribution does not require snappy slogans or eye catching packaging design. It does not create logos or TV ads. It involves a lot of long-term planning and co-ordination and so this is an often neglected segment of the overall marketing mix.

However, it forms an essential element of determining the strategic direction of an organisation – it can shape the entire format of the business and can truly be the driver of a business' ultimate success. It is, for this reason, that understanding marketing's role in planning business distribution is crucial for any organisation.

Chapter 1: What Does 'Distribution' Really Mean?

Distribution, within an organisation, relates to processes, people and interrelations between other organisations to connect the production of products and services to their end-users. It is a chain of elements that, when connected, provides a smooth flow of orders and fulfilment across the business. Like a chain it is as strong as the weakest link and it can be long and distributed or short and concise.

This book analyses and assesses the different distribution models and identifies the key issues related to determining distribution strategy across an organisation. The key areas examined are:

- National Distribution
- Distribution and the Product Mix
- Business to Business (B2B)
- Business to Consumer (B2C)
- Franchise
- Channel Churn, Inter-Channel Conflict, Cannibalisation and Margin Management
- International Distribution
- Direct Investment
- Partnerships, Distributors and Agents
- Brand and IPR Protection
- Legal Constraints
- Services Distribution
- Direct Service Distribution
- Indirect Service Distribution
- Electronic Distribution Models
- The Internet and Disintermediation of the Channel
- Free, Premium and Freemium Models

In general physical products and intangible services can be considered to be similar within the context of distribution.

Therefore this book sometimes refers to these two elements with the generic term 'products'. Where there are significant differences these are detailed.

Chapter 2: National Distribution

Almost without exception, an organisation begins by setting up within a single country and therefore national distribution is the starting point for any distribution model and hence this book. Many of the elements of distribution within a country or territory are common to International Distribution and so, to avoid duplication, are included only within the National Distribution chapters.

2.1 Distribution and the product mix

When assessing the distribution methods suitable for an organisation, the first element to consider is the Product Mix.

The product mix of an organisation will clearly affect the type and range of customers that will buy from them but in addition, the buyer behaviour towards those products will determine the best channel/channels of distribution for them.

As an example, if a company produced only plastic cable ties then its buyers would be a large range of people and organisations. However very few organisations have sufficient needs for cable ties for them to seek out and buy them direct from the manufacturer. With such a low net value and low margin commodity product, any savings from buying direct would be outweighed by the increased transaction costs of finding and negotiating a direct supply contract. Therefore unless the company were to branch out into a wider range of products (probably at great cost) then a direct manufacturer to end-user distribution model is unlikely to be suitable, requiring the use of a distribution chain to incorporate these products into the ranges of other sellers.

As a counter example, the Volkswagen Audi Group makes vehicles for virtually every market segment. It also owns Bugatti. Bugatti make one single model of car. Because this vehicle is so unique it is not necessary for Bugatti to have an entire range of vehicles, nor indeed a dealership chain, service facilities or any of the other elements usually required for an effective model range. The potential buyers of these vehicles are able and willing to bypass the normal motor vehicle "structure" and buy direct.

These two examples show that the product or service being offered affects the viability of different distribution models.

2.2 Distribution and the value chain

In general terms, it is possible to map the added value of the product or service to the complexity of the distribution chain. When the originating organisation is offering a commodity product with little intrinsic value then it is often necessary to use a distribution chain that can add value to that product or service. If the product is of high intrinsic value (not necessarily price) then it may be possible for the originator to remove large elements of the distribution chain.

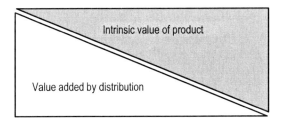

Figure 2.1 Intrinsic value vs value added

An example would be milk production – the core commodity is typically low price and relatively low value and so the farmers need to use a dairy co-operative to bulk up the volumes to then sell to a packaging/bottling dairy which then sells to the supermarkets. At each stage of the process value is added. The farmer has relatively little to differentiate his product, does not add significant unique value and so relies on others to generate the value.

An alternative route would be for the farmers to produce a higher quality product, then add value themselves (perhaps turning it into high quality cheese or ice-cream) and then sell this to specialist outlets directly. By adding value to the product they can remove layers of the distribution chain and internalise extra profits. This of course requires the product to be sufficiently well differentiated from other similar products to be able to justify the added value and costs.

In general as a product becomes a commodity then the value in that product reduces and so it is necessary to add value back into it. Organisations can attempt to add the value themselves or look towards a distribution channel to add its own value into the product.

2.3 Buyer behaviour

When considering the best distribution model for your products or services it is important to consider not only the capabilities of the organisation but also the buyer behaviour of the typical customer type. This can be analysed using the following criteria:

- Homogeneous or heterogeneous purchasing
- Brand visibility
- Discretionary vs. essential purchases
- Frequency – how often are the products or services purchased?

Homogeneous vs. heterogeneous purchasing

This is the clearest differentiator for the distribution model for products. Those products which are purchased almost exclusively without other products are usually candidates for a short simple distribution chain – for example cars or other very high value items. Those items which are usually bought with a "basket" of other goods, in particular food and other commodity items usually require a distribution chain that supports this level of aggregation. It is hard to imagine a shop selling nothing but milk being successful, as obviously the number of shoppers buying milk alone is low and the transaction cost of buying milk from the milk shop then going to the supermarket for the rest of the week's shopping is too high.

Brand visibility

The most obvious example of brand visibility is Apple – it is quite simply one of the biggest, best known and most valuable brands ever. With its core customer base virtually obsessed with the products and completely linked into the Apple "Ecosystem", Apple is able to virtually ignore the perceived wisdom of the technology markets it sells into, and indeed virtually every aspect of the marketing mix sees Apple as both a landmark organisation and a maverick!

A counter to this highly visible brand would be a book publishing imprint. Take a look at the spines of the books on your shelves and you will see many different publishing imprints. However, in terms of your buying behaviour, these brands are largely irrelevant. In many cases the author can be considered to be the brand rather than the publisher.

In most cases though, books tend to be sold in a brand-free environment within a mixed distribution channel (the key exceptions being educational books and 'Mills and Boon'). Even before Amazon, the concept of a single brand bookshop with a wholly owned and exclusive distribution channel would be hard to contemplate. A similar situation would be the music publishing industry. Partially because of the lack of brand visibility and the need to leverage third party distribution chains, these two industries have been notable for the number and scale of mergers and re-organisations as businesses struggle to adapt their business models.

Discretionary vs. essential purchases and frequency of purchase
These two elements are in many cases the weakest differentiators when defining the distribution chain. They are themselves closely linked and so have been combined here for simplicity. In essence they are delineators of 'Value' and 'Value Add'. Discretionary, infrequent purchases tend to be highly value-added whereas frequent, essential purchases tend to be low value add. Once again this will tend to define their idealised distribution chain along the same lines.

2.4 Competition
When a product is faced with substantial competition there are two diametrically different distribution strategies that can be taken. The first is to pursue a segregated strategy to clearly remove your product or service from the competition, whereas the other is to take competition head-on and allow the products to be directly compared 'on the shelves'.

An example of the first strategy would be Direct Line (www.directline.com) who, when faced with a highly competitive insurance marketplace made an explicit strategy to offer a direct only approach and not to use the distribution model of the price comparison websites. Direct Line uses this strategy as part of its overall communications and marketing approach to seek to demonstrate their difference and imply a cost benefit to the consumer by cutting out the middleman. They have applied this strategy for many years and so it would appear to work well, though at the cost of supporting their own (expensive) TV marketing spend rather than relying on the spend of the comparison services.

Again within the insurance industry, the converse strategy occurs with small, highly-focused insurance companies using the intermediary of the comparison websites to be able to compete with the larger, general purpose insurance companies. Here they have decided that the cost of using the distributor in terms of commission is much lower than the alternative costs of raising their brand visibility to enhance direct sales. In this example, they have measured the entry costs of both the direct and indirect sales channels and have decided on the indirect channel. This analysis demonstrates that the ideal distribution channel or channel mix is highly dependent on the product mix, the value chain and buyer behaviour.

Chapter 3: Business to Business Distribution
3.1 Factors affecting distribution strategies in B2B structures

Within the Business to Business (B2B) sector there are a number of key factors that differ from Business to Consumer (B2C) marketing and distribution. They are:

- Volume
- Value
- Margin
- Customer numbers
- Complexity

How these factors affect your business model will help to determine the distribution strategies best suited to your organisation.

Volume

Many B2B transactions are relatively high volume. This is particularly true of commodity products and component products. For most items in high volume B2B transactions there is little core value that can be added by intermediaries. Where value is added in these sectors, it tends to be in the areas of trading, particularly in supply and futures trading.

The buyers of many commodities require continuity of supply and assurance of price over the medium to long term and so will prefer to use trading markets to support their needs. These traders seek to add value to the transaction for both the supplier and the end customer by offering both parties continuity of sale and supply respectively, and certainty of price and cost. They use a variety of techniques for this including:

Forward contracts – these are agreements between two parties to exchange at some fixed future date a given quantity of a commodity for a price defined today. The fixed price today is known as the forward price.

Futures contracts – essentially, a futures contract is a standardised forward contract in which the buyer and the seller accept the terms in regards to product, grade, quantity and location and are only free to negotiate the price. This type of contract has been in place since the 17th Century though its use took hold in the USA in the 19th Century.

Hedging – a common practice in food commodities. A typical hedger might be a commercial farmer. The market values of wheat and other crops fluctuate constantly as supply and demand for them vary, with occasional large moves in either direction. Based on current prices and forecast levels at harvest time, the farmer might decide that planting wheat is a good idea one season, but the forecast prices are only that – forecasts. Once the farmer plants wheat, he is committed to it for an entire growing season. If the actual price of wheat rises greatly between planting and harvest, the farmer stands to make a lot of unexpected money, but if the actual price drops by harvest time, he could be ruined.

If at planting time, the farmer sells a number of wheat futures contracts equivalent to his anticipated crop size, he effectively locks in the price of *wheat* at that time: the contract is an agreement to deliver a certain number of bushels of wheat to a specified place on a certain date in the future for a certain fixed price. The farmer has hedged his exposure to wheat prices; he no longer cares whether the current price rises or falls, because he is guaranteed a price by the contract. He no longer needs to worry about being ruined by a low wheat price at harvest time, but he also gives up the chance of making extra money from a high wheat price at harvest times.

As a further derivative on these trading activities, it is possible to factor the anticipated payment of a futures contract thus converting an agreement to be paid in the future for an immediate payment (albeit at a reduced rate). This allows a commodity supplier to realise cash from business activities that may not have even commenced at the time of the contract. The risk involved in these secondary derivatives can be high and may need to be offset with a complex series of hedging agreements to cover the risk of non-delivery.

This complex range of activities is normally considered non-core to the business operations. However, they can dramatically alter the structure of the cost/value profile of the organisation. By using these intermediaries within the distribution chain between production and consumption, the profit structure of the business is affected. Many organisations can actually generate more profit from their futures trading and hedging activities than they make from the core business activities (Encana, 2012).

All of these financial-based activities rely on there being substantial volume requirements within the market for a product that is largely identical regardless of supplier, a significant number of suppliers and a significant number of buyers. Without these three elements, the scope for trading, offsetting and pre-selling of products is extremely limited.

Value
Where volume and commoditisation of the product does not apply then the value element of the product offering comes into play. Value in this sense relates significantly to uniqueness. Once again, as previously discussed, products with a low initial value need enhancement through the distribution chain whereas products with high value/uniqueness may not require this. Once again there are exceptions to this general principle which can be summarised in the following terms:

Locality – many B2B high value transactions require on-going support, maintenance, and aftercare and even within a national context, these services may be best supported by a localised organisation. Large capital equipment would be an example. Therefore the distribution chain is being used mainly for aftersales support of local customers.

Customisation – B2B high value transactions can often be typified by a degree of customisation that does not occur within the B2C sector. Many organisations may choose to defer this to other organisations so that they can focus on their core activities.

Integration – of particular interest within the IT/high technology sector, the integration of a range of different products and services from multiple suppliers is often required and can best be supported by a highly focused distribution channel.

Margin

Frequently linked to value and volume is the margin available on a product. The operation of a dedicated sales and marketing function is an expensive activity for any organisation and if the organisation has relatively few customers then this pro-rata cost can be high. It can therefore be worthwhile for an organisation to split this margin with the distribution channel and so access their sales functions.

Take the case of a B2B manufacturer of highly specialised, high value, high margin but low volume items. To maintain a national sales team which may only support 3–4 sales per quarter would be an expensive undertaking. However by using the sales channel of a distributor the direct sales costs can be reduced and the distributor would be able to incorporate this product into their portfolio. The manufacturer gains access to an established customer base without the costs of creating it. The distributor accepts a marginal additional cost whilst gaining the potential for extra sales and income.

Of course it is necessary to ensure that the distributor is committed to the product and is actively selling it: channel management is key.

Customer numbers

In general terms the number of customers a B2B business will manage is lower than the number a B2C business will handle and in general the length of the relationship will be longer. Also the transaction time will tend to be longer (time between first contact and first sale). Because of these factors, there will typically be more of a relationship between the supplier and the customer. These factors reduce the "distance" between them.

Many B2B companies will take advantage of the opportunity for focus that the small number of customers offers and seek to reduce the role of the distribution chain as far as possible.

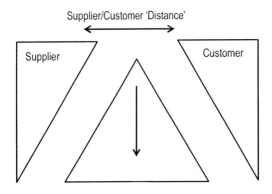

Increasing role of distribution

Figure 3.1. Role of distributor in connecting suppliers to customers

Complexity

As we move away from commodity suppliers the complexity of the goods or services increases. This can have two different effects on the position of the value chain and the distribution mode. If the products are extremely complex and require a consultative sale, commissioning and support process, the supplier organisation may choose to internalise all of this work. This approach is particularly effective if the contract involves almost exclusively one single supplier with a small number of minor sub-contractors and so the supplier and the purchaser may consider that prime contractor status is appropriate – with the prime contractor taking on the role of project manager.

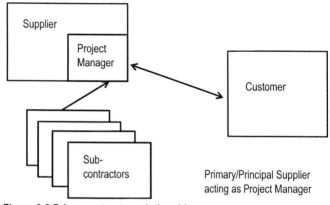

Figure 3.2 Prime contractor relationship

If the supplier's services are part of a wider system then the purchaser may prefer to devolve the contract to a third party that can act as a project/contract manager. This manager can then take the responsibility for negotiating with all the suppliers. In many cases these project managers will not expect to be paid from the suppliers' margins (in some cases this will be expressly prohibited) but will charge a premium to the customer.

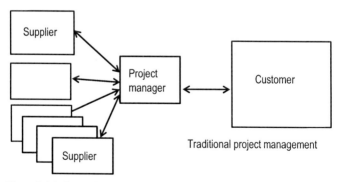

Figure3.3 Independent project manager relationship

In some cases a third approach may apply. In this circumstance the supplier would normally manage any sub-contractors themselves – however, due to the nature of the project and the lack of skills within the customer, the customer may appoint an external project manager to manage the interface with the supplier. The customer will put a value on avoiding complexity and will judge the value offered by a neutral third party in managing complexity compared with the estimated costs of managing the complexity internally.

An example of this third party management process can be seen with the Cambridge Guided Busway (a major infrastructure project local to Cambridge Marketing College). In this project, Cambridgeshire County Council opted to use a professional project management company (Atkins) to manage the prime contractor (BAM Nuttall). The costs of engaging a third party on this project were considered good value compared to the risks and internal cost of managing such a project.

This is of particular relevance as, in this case, the customer has little experience of infrastructure projects of this type and so the risks implied by managing the contract internally were considered to be high. In the end the project was nearly two years overdue and numerous legal cases are in progress relating to cost and time overruns and the role of the project manager so it is not clear if the use of a third party was appropriate (Wynne, 2012).

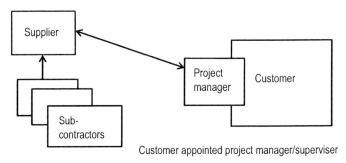

Customer appointed project manager/superviser

Figure 3.4. Customer appointed oversight

In summary the level of complexity of a solution and the relative experience of the supplier and customers can have a significant effect on the style of interface and the idealised distribution channel.

3.2 Distribution modes in B2B structures

Having assessed the factors that influence distribution strategies in the B2B sector it is now possible to analyse the different distribution modes that this sector can employ.

They break down into the following key areas:

- Direct
- Via subsidiary
- Direct fulfilment using agents
- Via distributor
- Via multi-tiered distribution

Direct

Clearly the simplest distribution mechanism and the solution that, due to not needing to pay any commission or fees, offers the highest gross margin.

Here all the sales and marketing functions are internalised within the selling business:

- All communication to the buyer is direct
- All marketing is undertaken by the selling organisation – albeit many organisations physically outsource at least some marketing activities (by which we mean all marketing is selected, commissioned, and paid for by the selling organisation)
- All order fulfilment is undertaken by the seller (excepting the actual physical distribution of items by lorry etc. which is usually outsourced!)

This format, of course, requires the selling organisation to be adept at all these functions. It needs a highly motivated sales and marketing department; it needs to fully understand the market place; it needs to understand the buyer requirements and it needs the ability to offer the full suite of fulfilment activities (order processing, manufacture, commissioning (if needed), and after sales support). This range of activities is extensive and for an organisation to be able to undertake all these functions is unusual.

The simplest analogy for this multi-function skill would be a cycling team (an image familiar to anyone who has watched the Olympics or the Tour de France). A cycling team needs to have a group of dedicated individuals all striving for the common purpose. Each member of the team takes their turn at the front of the pack, pulling the other team members along, then the next member takes over and contributes, followed by another and another all through the team. Only if each member contributes fully can the team win. Even if the team had a hugely skilled individual, if any member of the team turned up hung over or riding a penny farthing, then the team as a whole would fail.

With an organisation attempting every element of the fulfilment chain internally, there is both the risk of any one of the elements working sub-optimally and also the additional management costs of integrating all the functions.

It is necessary to critically assess the entire organisation to ensure that it is performing optimally. The skill sets required to develop and produce products and services are often different from those required to build an effective sales channel and so some organisations opt to develop a completely separate sales subsidiary to ensure management focus.

Use of a wholly owned sales subsidiary
This model is commonly used within international organisations but it occasionally occurs within a national structure as well. In many cases the production element and sales element are both owned by a separate holding company. In addition to the management focus this structure can offer, it also has a number of other benefits.

For example a manufacturing company may produce two lines which are focused on different customer bases or may have developed or acquired a line that has a different profile of customer. It may be decided that the new line would be better served by a more focused sales organisation (perhaps under a different brand) and so the sales of this range may be hived off to a separate organisation whilst maintaining the principle product (and/or brand) with the parent company.

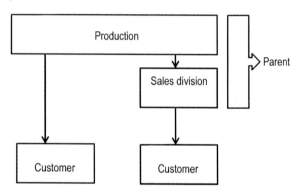

Figure 3.5 Multi-mode, multi-customer distribution

Alternatively the organisation may be considering a multi-mode sales model where it offers other companies access to its products whilst still wishing to sell the products itself. In order to ensure parity and a "Chinese Wall" between these two channels the organisation may decide to (or in some cases be forced to) set up a separate sales company. The largest and most visible example of this structure would be BT with its BT Openreach (building and supporting the infrastructure), BT Business, and BT Wholesale divisions. In this case the regulator insisted on this separation but many companies would set this structure up for themselves.

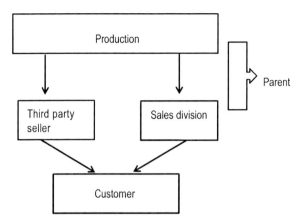

Figure 3.6 Multi-mode, homogenous customer distribution

Another environment where this approach occurs is within the petrol supply industry. Organisations may own the oil exploration and distribution elements of the business within one company (refining tends to be outsourced in a complex set of business structures, beyond the scope of this Handbook) and may, through a separate company, own a chain of branded petrol stations. It may also sell its fuels through a set of franchised petrol stations which, although they carry the same branding, will be independent businesses operating through a completely separate channel within the parent company.

One example of this structure is BP. Its own petrol stations can be identified by the use of the "Wild Bean Cafe" brand for its own coffee/refreshments whereas the franchise operations may offer different coffee brands (Costa or Coffee Nation are common). The brand of coffee on sale is often the only way to distinguish which are owned and which are franchised. This dual supply structure will sometimes allow BP to 'own' a near monopoly on petrol supply in an area whilst avoiding any competition rulings.

This structure shows one other possible reason for the use of a wholly owned subsidiary: the taxation and funding advantages that may accrue from such a structure. Manufacturing can be capital intensive and may require complex loan and hedging financial structures, whereas a B2B sales and marketing structure can be relatively low cost and is more straight forward to finance. By splitting a business into two legally separate entities the organisation can take advantage of different funding routes – borrowing cheaply using the lower risk entity and cross-subsidising the higher risk entity by either inter-division financing or other structures, such as paying higher than market rate for goods; buying 'consultancy services' from the other entity: management fees, licence fees, etc. Again the complexities of intra-company financing are beyond the scope of this Handbook but these structures can offer significant funding advantages.

Other advantages come from tax allowances against research and development fees. By separating the income element (the sales activities) from the cost element (R&D, and/or manufacturing) and providing multiple reimbursement methods between the two organisations (such as consultancy, licensing, management fees, etc.), it is possible to gain advantages on corporation tax, VAT and other taxes.

Fulfilment by agents
Agents (usually self-employed sales people) are a diminishing element of the distribution chain in many developed countries. Their usefulness has been surpassed by manufacturers bypassing them and selling direct to the end business (often through telesales or on-line processes). This offers the business a reduced cost of entry into sales markets compared to the costs of recruiting, training and paying commissions to agents.

Sales agents do not normally work within the contract chain (all contracts, payments and deliveries are conducted between the supplier and the customer). Though some agents may very occasionally accept payments, subtract their commission and pay the remainder on to the supplier, this is very much the exception (certainly within the national structures).

One area where an agency is still active is in parts of the independent retail sector (and in particular, toys). This sector still has a significant number of very small retailers – many of whom will stock many hundreds (if not thousands) of lines from many manufacturers. Some parts of the business still rely on a personal touch (soft toys in particular are rarely bought without seeing samples) so neither telesales nor online fulfilment are practical. Yet the diffuse nature of the retailers and their individual small order size (minimum order values of less than £250 are common) make in-house physical sales agents unprofitable. In this case the use of agents – most of whom will be multi-supplier agents – offers the manufacturers significant advantages.

These agents can visit the retailers, demonstrate new lines and will often undertake merchandising and stock replenishment orders for the retailer. Even though the agent may only earn £20–£30 per manufacturer per visit in commission they may service 3–5 lines with each retailer making the visit cost-effective for them. The retailers value this personal touch as often the agent will recommend different lines to the retailer based on their experience at other sites and may suggest complementary products from other manufacturers.

Distributors
Beyond the basic function of the agents come distributors. Distributors can in some cases still be individuals though by taking on the ordering, fulfilment, invoicing and payment collection, they are expanding their role in the chain. Most distributors will be small to medium sized companies – again offering multiple lines to 'the trade'. Again there are exceptions. Computacenter.com is a £2.5 billion turnover organisation and, within the IT sector, distributors of this size are not infrequent.

The distinction between distributors and wholesalers is often made in that wholesalers will place orders 'on spec' and then aim to sell on those products to other organisations (Booker food distribution would be an example), whereas distributors normally do not hold stock but act more like an outsourced sales entity – passing on customer orders on a 1-to-1 ratio. Again this split applies in the majority of cases, though in some areas, distributors may hold significant stocks of common basic items to ensure rapid turnaround of orders.

Once again wholesalers and distributors aim to offer a wider range of products and services to their customers than a single manufacturer can support. This allows the buyer to reduce their transaction costs substantially compared to buying from the individual suppliers. (Hennart, 2010) In many cases the cost of selecting, contracting, negotiating and processing the orders can be so substantial that buyers will pay a premium for products purchased through a trusted distributor.

Multi-tiered distribution

Multi-tiered distribution is relatively rare within the national environment as it tends to require a degree of complexity that is not typical within a national environment. One area where this multi-tier model operates is within car spare parts. Unipart acts as a distributor for many different OEM (original equipment manufacturer) parts as well as unbranded or generic items for the motor trade. It will purchase the components typically either from the manufacturer direct or, in the case of many non-current vehicles, from a subsidiary then sell these through to its own franchise operations, and motor repair chains. The franchises will then act as distributors to the smaller independent garages who use the items. This is an example of both a multi-tier distribution chain and an internalised distribution arm within the same organisation. The complexity of this chain is only matched by the amazing flexibility, with spare parts ordered in the morning by the garage being delivered in many cases within 4–5 hours by the local franchise with overnight replenishment undertaken by the higher tiers of the chain.

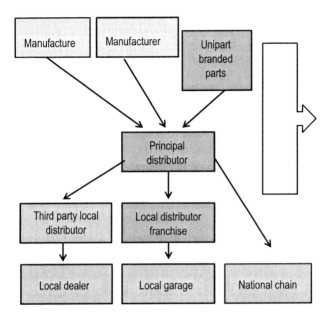

Figure 3.7 Multi-tiered distribution

Summary

What can be learnt from this group of distribution schema? The primary conclusion is that there are almost as many different variations of schema as there are companies. Generalisation is hard and largely fruitless. However there is one commonality that the majority of these methods share – value to the customer.

3.3 Value to the customer

With the exception of the complex financially derived models of some companies, all these models are focused on delivering the maximum value to the customer and this is a common theme throughout marketing.

In order to determine the best distribution structure for your organisation it is first necessary to ignore the needs of your company and put yourself into the mind of the buyer. What is the buyer's idealised distribution model? How do they work? What works for them?

In the vast majority of cases, any organisation will be operating in a highly competitive environment. Competitors will be fighting to capture market share and/or profitability. If your organisation is not structured in the most suitable way for your customers then the likelihood is that a competitor will be.

Customers in general, and business customers in particular, are looking for the simplest, least hassle approach to supply. By simplifying their supply side requirements, less time and energy is spent on the "cost" side of their business and so proportionally more can be spent on the "income" side. This double saving provides a huge incentive to the buying company to find a supply partner that does what they want them to do.

Of course this idealised supply side model may not be as profitable as the perfect production-focused model. It may require extra stock holding, the use of distributors which reduce gross margin, the provision of local presence that may not be optimal, and many other factors.

A practical distribution model is therefore a hybrid between the supply side and production models. However any compromise away from the supply side model should be carefully considered to ensure that this is not offering your competitors an advantage.

Chapter 4: Business to Customer Distribution
4.1 Differences between B2B and B2C

The primary differences between B2B and B2C activities are:

- size;
- diffusion; and
- margin.

Size

Almost by definition the consumer market is significantly larger than the B2B market in almost every sector. The consumer market can be 10, 100 even 1,000 times larger than any given B2B sector. Each 10 tonne lorry of grain sold to a major factory baker is turned into 50,000 loaves of bread and is sold to about 15,000 families a week. The demand for basic sliced bread in the UK (60,000,000 people) is supplied by less than 20 industrial sized bakery businesses implying a virtually 3,000,000 to 1 ratio of manufacturers to customers. Few other industries have such an extreme manufacturer to customer ratio, though Apple, with 5 million iPhones sold in less than a week is probably another extreme example!

Manufacturers of volume consumer items will often consider sales volumes in the order of millions and rarely less than the 100,000s. However, at the opposite extreme are specialist and luxury brands that sell in volumes of 100–1000.

Diffusion

Of course one problem with these huge potential and actual customer volumes is that they are diffuse. This refers to geographic and demographic spread. This has implications for both physical distribution and also the need to communicate to this customer base. The opportunities and complexities generated by a large, diffuse customer base colour the distribution model options to a large degree.

Margin

Manufacturing for and selling to the end user represents the maximisation of margin across the sales process – essentially B2C counts the entirety of the margin between retail prices and cost of production. The downside is that it also incorporates the entirety of the cost of sale. This covers every aspect of all elements of sales and physical distribution and also all brand building, product marketing and promotion for the product and any general marketing costs for the manufacturer. Encompassing the entire margin looks initially attractive but having to absorb the entire cost chain may be less so.

4.2 End-to-end distribution

Coupled with the costs of attempting to manage the whole distribution chain there is, in many cases, the sheer impossibility of doing so. A major sliced bread manufacturer would not attempt to sell directly to its customers even though there are about 60,000,000 of them in the UK. Not just because the costs of setting up shops in high streets to sell the products would be unsustainable (they probably would be), but because the buying behaviour for the products is such that it makes approach impossible. Sliced bread, a commodity, is purchased in conjunction with a (literal) basket of other products and so any customer is highly unlikely to visit a separate store to purchase it. It would, of course, be theoretically possible for all major bread manufacturers to simultaneously refuse to supply the supermarkets and force buyers to buy directly from them. This would be impossible to manage as to do so would either require (illegal) collusion or would put manufacturers at the risk of one breaking ranks and going back to selling to the supermarkets. Bread is such a low margin product (in some cases even a loss-leading item), that in any case there would be no benefit in the manufacturers attempting such an action.

Consumer commodities such as bread, etc. are an unusual case. There is very little value added to the product itself throughout the distribution chain. The margin on the product is extremely small and remains small throughout the chain. Where this type of product adds its value is in its combination with other products in the basket and by being an 'essential'.

Supermarkets expend large floor areas on sliced bread and milk. The margins earned per square metre by that part of the floor are tiny compared to that earned by other areas of the supermarket (wines, etc.). However, their presence is essential. No-one would ever contemplate running a supermarket without bread because virtually no customers would ever shop there.

These products are considered to be 'pull-through' products as they pull the customers through the doors. These are almost passive product sales – added to the shopping list and basket almost without thinking and this is reflected in the very limited advertising that takes place for these products.

Most non-food products do not fit into this description and demand has to be generated through some form of consumer marketing.

Marketing across the retail distribution channel takes two clear forms:

- Demand marketing
- Supplier marketing

4.3 Demand marketing

Demand Marketing is, as the name suggests, focused on persuading customers to purchase a particular product. This marketing can be either brand switching or demand generation marketing. It is usually solely organised by the manufacturers and in most cases is cross channel. Occasionally joint marketing will take place to tie the increased demand with a source of supply.

Many larger retail chains will refuse to accept a new product (or order large quantities of an existing product) without the assurance of a substantial amount of demand marketing taking place.

Timing of this marketing is essential. Too early and demand exists for a product that is not available; too late and the stockists have stock on shelves for an extended period of time with little demand. Most retailers will expect to sell a sufficient volume and value of the stock to pay for the entire order before the invoice is due to be paid and so marketing needs to be in place to assist in this aim. Awareness of the lag between consumer marketing and actual demand is crucial. Managing the marketing effort to tie with stock availability of new products is a careful balancing act between these three variables.

Each member of the chain between the manufacturer and the customer will need a different marketing message and activity to ensure that supply of goods or services through the chain matches demand.

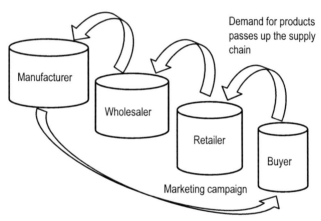

Demand for products passes up the supply chain

Manufacturer

Wholesaler

Retailer

Buyer

Marketing campaign

Figure 4.1 Push marketing – demand generation

4.4 Supplier marketing
Supplier marketing is, put simply, the marketing between the retail end of the supply chain and their customers to persuade consumers to make them the supplier of choice. It can also be termed Fulfilment Marketing.

This marketing is often product neutral or may involve multiple products from multiple upstream suppliers. This type of marketing divorces, to an extent, the brand of the product from the supply of the product and can have the effect of **Brand Dilution**.

Examples of this would be supermarket food retailers seeking to make shoppers come to their shops instead of competitor shops. The brands of the products sold are largely irrelevant. Brand Dilution is a significant issue with many products and services sold via a long distribution channel. Customers see the brand of the seller and make associations with that brand rather than that of the product.

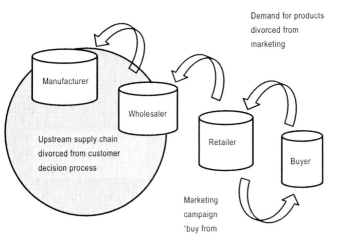

Figure 4.2 Supplier marketing

It is for this reason that many premium brands opt for a branded sales strategy – either with their own outlets or by using a franchise model. Much clothing is sold in this manner and many high end luxury items are also sold from a branded chain (Swarovski and Apple are key examples in the premium non-clothing arena with organisations such as Lush and The Body Shop operating at a lower price/margin point). In this way the brand values can be maintained through the distribution chain.

This brand protection has obvious limits:

- The product must have high enough demand and margin to support the overheads of a dedicated presence
- The product must be a 'solo' product – needing no supporting unbranded products. (Interestingly Apple stores also stock a small range of non-Apple accessories in recognition of the need for some supporting products (or perhaps to internalise the profits from some of these add-on sales.)
- It must be possible to support sufficient coverage of the marketplace easily

Relatively few non-clothing brands can support this level of coverage and even some clothing brands have difficulty supporting own-brand stores. This generates a market for the in-store franchise within department stores. These franchises offer a marginal compromise to the issue of brand dilution with the ability to provide some aspects of the brand whilst benefiting from the footfall of the department store and the reduction in fixed costs. The department stores benefit from this association with third party brands and uses them as 'pull-through' brands in store to raise their own profile.

A primary example would be the perfume and cosmetics brands within Department Stores. These brands act to draw consumers into the store which then aims to persuade customers to buy other products at the same time. Within this example the brands of the perfume and cosmetics are acting as the draw for the customers.

A customer chooses to buy Chanel perfume based on their marketing – the venue for that transaction (a department store) is largely irrelevant.

An interesting question then arises in these stores regarding the placement of the cosmetics counters. By being in the front of the store (as seems to be traditional) the opportunity to persuade customers to 'reach' further into the store for other products seems limited and so the marketing leverage the department store gains from hosting the perfume counter would seem to be limited.

4.5 B2C services distribution

The market for B2C services is wide and diverse – from mortgages, banking, and insurance to mobile phone contracts. Excluding mortgage payments it is estimated that 20% of all consumer spending is on intangible services (ONS, 2012). This market is dominated largely by a direct marketing approach though significant inroads are being made by on-line price comparison sites. As the need for physical delivery of items is unnecessary, online direct sales is a highly scalable model for this business.

Areas of B2C activity that can be seen to be migrating to a service model are the areas of music, video and books. Each of these fields is taking advantage of the reduction in costs through electronic distribution (in both production and maintenance of a distribution channel), and the increased flexibility of purchasing that the new consumer technologies offer. Ebook downloads in terms of value have now (Q3, 2012) exceeded hardback sales, in the USA (Publishing Perspectives, 2012) and this trend is accelerating.

Music has virtually disappeared as a physical retail product and video and PC gaming are only continuing due to the current lack of electronic distribution infrastructure. Console gaming still largely requires physical media for Digital Rights Management (DRM) purposes but this area and also video are moving to an on-line sales with physical distribution through postal services.

It is interesting to note that music distribution has moved much more quickly into a predominantly on-line model with downloads onto dedicated music devices (or increasingly mobile devices such as smartphones), whereas the majority of video distribution has focused on rental/streaming of videos, with physical sales of DVDs still significant. This is primarily due to the large scale penetration of devices able to permanently store the extremely large files required for HD or 3D full-length movies. Because of this and the lack of penetration of ultra-high-speed broadband services, DVD sales have been less affected to date by on-line services.

Banking is increasingly moving to an electronic model (with increasing focus on mobile) and in many countries even many government services are, or are planned to move, online.

Mobile commerce is becoming a major industry with mobile devices (smart phones and tablets) becoming highly focused media consumption devices (as opposed to PCs which are being increasingly relegated to workplace items). Mobile users (mainly apple iOS and Android) were downloading nearly 1 billion apps a week in the first quarter of 2012 (Reilly, 2012) and as an industry this market is continuing to grow apace. However not all of these apps are the end result and many are now used as an intermediary for other service sales. These include banking apps, on-line shopping applications (eBay for example) and even travel applications (Trainline and Ryanair in the UK) allowing tickets to be purchased and timetables examined.

It is an interesting development which, unfortunately, is beyond the scope of this Handbook, that computing devices in the home are dramatically shifting their focus away from home focused office productivity devices onto a separate family of products that have limited production capabilities (beyond pictures and video) and are almost completely targeted at consuming media.

This proliferation of consumption devices is not only changing the market for home electronics but is also changing the distribution mechanism and mode for a large number of consumer services. For example, as the penetration of mobile smartphone and tablet devices increases, organisations are focusing much of their delivery towards them. NatWest in the UK has developed a dedicated banking application and heavily markets this as the primary interface for the majority of day-to-day banking. Paypal now offers a much closer integration to mobile phones and the Barclays Pingit service allows payments directly from phone to phone. (Interestingly the ability to transfer money from mobile phone to mobile phone to split the cost of a meal was the original driver behind PayPal.)

The proliferation of mobile consumer devices affected the business models of many media companies that rely on advertising to support free services.

Both Google and Facebook (Segall, 2012) found difficulties in maintaining revenues from these consumption devices as their mobile focused apps lacked the ability (and most importantly screen space) to host the paid for adverts that generate revenues. However, organisations such as Whatsapp moved directly into an explicit paid for model for their application to bypass the need to find mechanisms for paid adverts. Currently nearly 40% of consumer internet access is via mobile devices (phones or tablets) (Sterling, 2013) and so these devices are increasingly used for leisure access (including buying) in parallel with other media forms.

Any organisation considering the distribution of services into the consumer marketplace therefore has to consider these platforms as part of their overall marketing *and* delivery mechanism.

This level of mobile device marketing has a number of key characteristics that differentiate it from other marketing activities above and beyond the gross physical differences in format. These are:

Multi-mode – many mobile devices are used simultaneously with other media types. 25% of smartphone or tablet users will use them at the same time as watching the TV. This allows marketers to take advantage of this and incorporate interactivity between the device and the TV programme. Of course the TV programme has to stand alone to support more passive viewers but can offer supplementary services to this media grouping.

Reduced lag – because these devices are 'always on' users can quickly access websites which are promoted on TV ads, radio or even bus stop posters. This reduced lag has been mainly used to increase throughput of traditional marketing but some marketers are using this for extremely time sensitive advertising (spot betting during half-time ad breaks of football is an example). Time restricted special offers could be seen as the next logical step. By imposing a sense of urgency the buying decision can be condensed and the opportunities for comparison shopping reduced. Many sporting events on TV now have substantial adverts for real-time betting using apps downloaded onto phones.

Mobility – most street side advertising is focused at general awareness simply because the opportunity for fulfilment is not available. The use of mobile devices could alter this. As an (theoretical) example bus stop advertising could be used to target music downloads or other e-distributed products. By focusing adverts on bus stops near schools/ sixth forms with age related information and offering an e-fulfilment process direct to the mobile device, market penetration could be enhanced. This could cover not only music but mobile gaming or even sexual education/health advice direct to the target market (mobile equipped teenagers waiting for the bus home).

Micro-payments – most consumers will have some form of micro-payment mechanism implemented on their device (either iTunes or Google playstore) and so low value (<£5) payments are easy and quick to make and are virtually 'pocket money'. This makes the type of item able to be fulfilled through this device clearly defined. This type of service may render the currently moribund magazine market obsolete (or reinvigorated depending on your views) with e-magazines taking over from traditional paper distribution.

Chapter 5: Franchising

Franchise business models have frequently offered a very flexible distribution mechanism with a number of key benefits for both the Franchiser and Franchisee.

5.1 Franchising explained

Franchising is a huge industry and has been covered in great detail in a wide variety of books (nearly 1,300 are in print and on sale on Amazon) and so it would be impossible to do it full justice in a single chapter of this Handbook. However it is, in principle, a relatively simple system. An organisation has an idea or business that they have been able to prove to be successful. Usually this business will be some form of service business (fast food, office support, home services etc. are common). This type of business requires local distribution and support with local offices, shops, and/or staff.

In a widely distributed territory it would be extremely expensive to build the geographic spread of outlets necessary. The USA unsurprisingly is a major hub for franchising due to the huge geographical spread. Therefore the organisation develops a Franchise Model.

Within the franchise model various elements of the business are licensed to the franchisee. This includes the business name, branding, specialised equipment and designs for outlet fitting. Other elements may also be licensed, for example branded vehicles may be leased to the franchisee (either directly from the franchiser or through a leasing arrangement they have negotiated with a finance company). Supplies and raw materials may be supplied directly or again via purchasing deals set up for the purpose. High street examples of franchise operations include Thorntons' Chocolates and The Body Shop. In both cases it can be extremely difficult to identify the difference between a franchise and wholly-owned operation. As previously mentioned petrol stations are also frequently franchised operations with most petrol companies operating two separate and competing business structures for the different station types.

Accounts and management software and hardware (tills etc.) will normally be supplied (this is primarily to ensure the franchiser can monitor the business and reduce training costs). Training on running the business will be provided and other business training may also be offered at reduced rates.

The franchiser will be tasked with undertaking any national or global branding, to support the brand and to work to continually develop the business strategy.

The franchisee will usually pay an initial licence fee, plus royalties based on either sales, turnover or (less usually) profit. Many well established and popular franchises will charge extremely high initial fees (partly because demand is high and partly to ensure that the franchiser has an incentive to succeed in the long term.) Many will have relationships with finance companies (or may indeed own a finance company) who can offer the prospective franchisee loans to cover these fees which they can pay back over a period of time (alongside the annual fees).

This splitting of the business into a franchiser and multiple franchisees of course reduces the potential net margin available to the primary. However, the key benefits offered are leveraging and risk dilution.

Leverage
By focusing the funds of the franchiser on the development of the business concept and using franchisee funds to develop the distribution channel the franchiser can leverage their capital to deliver a business far faster than they would otherwise be able to. Without this leverage the franchiser would need to spread its funds into both developing the business and building the distribution – probably to the detriment of both.

Risk dilution
Within any business, there are many risks that can cause the business to fail. With a distributed business there are many risks that are unique and particularly higher in the early stages. The business model itself

may be sound but the location where the first outlets were placed may have been problematic, the store/outlet managers may not have been effective, etc. In addition, the cost of marketing the business may have a substantial fixed cost element making it almost as expensive to market a 10 outlet business as a 100 outlet business. A franchise model allows much more rapid expansion of the business to rapidly climb out of this risky early stage and become more quickly established. This can reduce and spread the risk more effectively.

Mixed mode franchise model

Many businesses will have a mixed mode franchise system where some outlets will be owned by the franchiser (possibly through a wholly owned subsidiary) whilst others will be owned through franchisees. This can result in forms of inter-channel conflict with wholly owned outlets being seen as competitors of the franchised outlets. This competition can result in cannibalisation of sales between these two groups and a lack of focus on external competitors.

This is a particular risk within the franchisee part of the business. As each franchise is a separate company (often private and family owned) it is very tempting for these businesses to be primarily focused on their own success and only secondarily concerned with the overall success of the franchise. Therefore there is no incentive for the franchisees to cede sales to other parts of the organisation. However as franchisees are ultimately responsible for their own success they frequently have a greater incentive to work hard to achieve this compared to salaried staff (even managerial staff) within company owned outlets.

Consequently, if a mixed mode model is used, it is necessary to recognise, understand and combat any possible inter-channel conflicts. This can take many forms but one of the principal forms is to ensure significant geographical distance between outlets to minimise conflicts. Other considerations can include:

- Incentives for managerial staff (as a minimum) within company outlets to enable them to benefit from success

- Ensuring pricing is managed to reduce cannibalisation through discounts
- Ensuring both franchise and owned outlets conform to the same standards of behaviour
- Ensuring a conflict resolution system exists and is seen to be fair

The most common sector which suffers from conflict within the mixed mode systems is the fuel retail business. Because the wholly owned operations do not need to make margins on fuel sales within the retail arm (relying on cross-subsidy from margins within the wholesale division) it can be possible for price conflicts to occur with nearby wholly owned operations seeking to cannibalise sales from the local franchise. This activity can be extremely counter-productive and is worsened by the separate business structures and reporting chains developed for each arm of the business.

5.2 Marketing a franchise distribution model
In many senses the marketing of a franchise scheme is relatively straightforward in the sense of the outward marketing of the business. Many franchise models are structured so that it is virtually impossible for the typical customer to recognise that the franchise exists. Most franchise structures have common standards across their outlets and many will have an overarching web and call centre operation that handles the majority of queries and then forwards these to an outlet for fulfilment.

This centralised model will constitute a significant overhead for the primary and so would need to be factored into the overall business model.

The alternative approach would be to rely on each outlet to undertake their own marketing directly. In some circumstances this may be a more appropriate model (particularly if services are extremely localised and specialised), however it would normally result in a net increase in the cost of marketing for the business as a whole. In addition each local franchise may have only limited marketing skills resulting in an overall sub-optimal marketing effort for the organisation. Business types where this localised marketing has been shown to be sustainable are mainly specialised B2C organisations (ranging from greetings cards to beauty products) where much of the selling activity occurs face-to-face (for example at gift fairs, etc.) and so centralised marketing would be superfluous.

Most B2C businesses (particularly high-street based) rely on centralised marketing to deliver brand awareness and then passing trade to capture customers. For example franchises such as McDonald's require very little localised marketing relying solely on centralised marketing activities.

Within the B2B community a larger amount of localised marketing may be required. These franchises often rely on a higher level of localised knowledge of the market, personal networking and personal recommendation rather than brand marketing.

A combination approach is often used for more generalised B2B services (printing, cartridge refill, vending machines, cleaning, etc.) where a level of general brand awareness is often required to differentiate between outwardly similar commodity services whilst local marketing is then used to fulfil the demand generated.

In summary the overall business strategy of franchised operations can invoke many different models and the marketing strategy needs to recognise these differences and react to them.

Added complexity
Marketing within a franchise can often be seen as similar to that used within a distributed channel operation with a range of added complexities around the areas of:

- **Brand management** – ensuring franchises have suitable tools to maintain and market the brand and have incentives to promote it
- **Channel conflict** – in multi-mode operations
- **Demand creation, demand fulfilment** – splitting these two elements can be problematic

- **Central vs. local marketing** – particularly where the local franchise may have limited marketing ability

5.3 Difficulties faced within channel management

Whenever a business model uses multiple organisations to fulfil the value cycle there exists a greater risk of conflict and difficulties. In essence these result from each organisation within the value chain having a different goal and focus and a different view of the priorities of the organisation as a whole. The key issues faced are:

- Channel churn
- Inter and intra– channel conflict
- Cannibalisation
- Margin management

Channel churn

Just as selling to a new customer is harder than selling to an existing customer, building a relationship with a downstream channel can be a lengthy and expensive process and it is therefore important to ensure that any downstream sellers are selected carefully and maintained. Brand loyalty amongst the channel is usually average to poor unless the products are highly in demand and unique with little opportunity for swap-out. For example:

- Wholesalers have very little interest in maintaining the profitability of the brand as a whole – their primary interest is ensuring profitable and rapid turnover of stock. Lines that do not provide sufficient turnover of stock will be dropped or maintained on a "special order" basis with the wholesaler acting as a "dropshipper" for the supplier. Most wholesalers will be seeking to minimise the time goods spend on their shelves (dwell time) and so focus on items that are actively demanded by their customers.

- Value added resellers have a greater interest in maintaining a brand over the medium to long-term but are largely seeking an overall profitable business model and may be willing to sacrifice products to maintain a high rate of return or may be willing to discount some products heavily in order to secure an overall profitable contract
- Independent retailers are usually seeking a high average turnover from the shelf space allocated to a product and are usually quick to discount to clear slow stock, move stocks to different areas of the store to enhance sales, and are willing to drop ranges that do not perform (or have given no signs of improved performance)
- Large retail chains will often require massive commitment for marketing activity yet may not be equally willing to support products if sales do not meet initial predictions

Many manufacturers have been severely affected by the tactics of large retailers. The perceived kudos of selling into these large retailers can often lead to new and inexperienced sellers agreeing to a very one-sided contractual agreement with commitment to marketing and promotions not being matched by equal commitment to product positioning and promotion. Many large retailers will negotiate one-sided payment terms with long credit terms (90–120 days not uncommon) and punitive sale or return agreements. Some even charge for products to be included within stock management systems or for the manufacturer to be included within the invoice payment system. This combination of terms seeks to divert all the risk of a product back to the manufacturer with the retailer retaining little or no risk.

As a corollary to this behaviour many independents will actively seek out products that are not stocked by the large chains (or Amazon) so that they can maintain their differentiation from chain stores and protect margins that would be at risk if chain stores (with their enhanced buying power) stocked the same products.

> This can result in the situation circumstance that when a supplier acquires a chain store stockist independents may drop or scale back on ranges. If the chain store then drops the product it will be hard (if not impossible) to persuade the independents to stock the product again. This occurred with a small toy manufacturer – Canterbury Bears – which originally focused on selling to small independent toy and gift shops. When it was acquired by Gund this strategy changed to supplying higher volumes to chain stores. The small retailers reacted by dropping the line and when the larger retailers moved to purchasing from China, Canterbury Bears found it had lost its market within the smaller retailers and the business folded.

The result of these issues is that a manufacturer has to select and manage its distribution channels carefully to minimise churn. It needs to:

- Ensure that the channels recruited are committed to the product and its success
- Ensure that the demand generation marketing is designed to direct customers towards the selected channel
- Support the channel with suitable, targeted, specific marketing
- Develop a long-term relationship with the channel
- Ensure that the product has sufficient strengths and 'uniqueness' to reduce the risk of the channel switching to competitive brands
- Manage the channel to enhance 'partnership'
- Ensure that any channel recruitment does not conflict with the aims of the existing channel or that, if there is conflict, there is a plan to manage this conflict

Inter and intra-channel conflict and cannibalisation
Intra-channel conflict most frequently occurs within the retail sector as different sellers of the same product make different pricing or promotion decisions in order to maximise their share of the market.

In relatively stable markets, price competition and promotions are designed to switch market share from one brand to another. Examples in the retail space would be washing powders/liquids or soft drinks. In these markets it is not possible to increase the overall size of the market dramatically and so activity is focused on capturing the market from competitors.

However, in markets where multiple sellers of the same product operate, many sellers will find it easier not to persuade buyers to switch products but instead to switch between sellers. An example may be within high street stores for consumer electrical goods or between on-line and high street sellers of the same product.

A particular issue within this on-line and high street channel conflict occurs with Amazon. Amazon now have an app which allows users to scan the barcodes on items they find in stores to find out if the same product is available via Amazon. Clearly this demonstrates significant and potentially disruptive conflict between channels as Amazon is using the power of the internet to effectively borrow the high street presence of their competitors as a free shop window to allow their customers to browse products without buying. It is unclear how a channel can be managed to avoid this level of conflict (particularly as retail price maintenance is illegal in most developed countries).

Retail Price Maintenance is a policy whereby the supplier attempts to fix the retail price of the goods its distributors sell. This can be via either explicit contract terms or by 'punishing' retailers that discount by limiting supply of goods or refusing to supply goods. Many companies will attempt to influence the retail price of goods in order to maintain a premium marketing position. The Net Book Agreement is a primary example of a Retail Price Maintenance policy.

The potential issues relating to intra-channel conflict within a franchise environment have been discussed previously but are particularly acute in circumstances where franchises have wide geographical territories and particularly in tight economic environments.

This can lead to franchises being 'flexible' or 'generous' in identifying the location of a customer (especially for B2B services or for 'at home' B2C sales) resulting in potentially significant conflicts.

These conflicts are more usually resolved by effective channel management, training and support, though the process can be assisted by effective marketing support to minimise the need for conflict.

In essence channel conflict largely occurs within static or mature markets. The key to controlling this conflict is therefore to either attempt to grow the marketplace (through either market or new product development) and so minimise the need to compete internally, or to control the supply to the channel and the channel size so that it accurately matches the demand. Imagine you are running a zoo with a lion enclosure. The lions are your sellers and the enclosure is the market. If your lions are breeding you will quickly find a need to expand the enclosure (the market) or control the numbers of lions (constraining the number of sellers) otherwise conflict will swiftly ensue!

With any channel it is crucial that the sales and marketing department places significant effort on the management of any reseller channels to ensure that the supply side of the channel is matched to the demand side. This can take the form of the following actions:

- Market analysis
- Size
- Profile
- Profitability
- Channel analysis
- Type
- Skills

Channel partners that no longer fit the model need either to be retrained, re-purposed or dropped to ensure that the channel is fit for purpose.

A distribution channel is equivalent to a flow of water from bucket to bucket – it is essential that each bucket in the chain is of the right type and capacity to match the flow of business through the channel.

Figure 5.1: The trickle-down flow of business through a distribution channel

5.4 Franchising in the retail sector and on-line fulfilment

One interesting aspect of the changes within the retail sector has been the reduction of the influence of the high street in the face of on-line B2C sales. For many branded retailers the high street presence is being restricted to being little more than a showroom where people browse products and then purchase them on-line. Apple with their Genius Bar and many demonstration units recognise the high street as being largely a showroom and aftersales support area which is supporting the on-line and third party sales of their products.

If the retailer owns both the high street presence and the on-line fulfilment structures then this model is sustainable with the cost of the high street presence being able to be offset by the on-line sales generated through this browsing. This internal cannibalisation is acceptable provided the company recognises the continued value of the high street as a marketing activity supporting the on-line operation.

However within the franchise model the ownership of the high street and the on-line fulfilment is split making these franchises less profitable for their owners. Any organisation with a franchise operation which is considering on-line operations should be aware of this risk of cannibalisation and put mechanisms in place to avoid it.

Chapter 6: International Distribution
6.1 The drivers for international expansion

Once an organisation has built a stable national base, many will start to look overseas for additional markets. The reasons behind looking internationally can often be summarised as follows:

- **Market saturation** – the national market has become saturated and further growth is either difficult/impossible or only achievable at great expense. An example of this would be the utility markets where European companies have found the stability and centralised control of their own markets a hard environment in which to create expansion and so have moved into the less constrained UK markets in order to enable expansion.

- **Competition** – again similar to market saturation, the business finds that the rate of growth of the business has tailed off due to competitors being more adept at capturing a large proportion of the growth potential. This reason is much weaker than saturation as it is predicated on the business already being weaker than its national competitors. Being weaker than your national competitors, where a business has the advantage of local knowledge, would suggest that entry into a foreign market with established competitors and without that local knowledge would be a risky option.

- **Expansion** – many organisations which are still growing in their base country wish to accelerate their growth by entering into new territories. These organisations often wish to leverage the skills and expertise gained within their home country. Many will use the expansion into other countries as an outlet for internally trained staff. Within a single country the typical pyramid structure of an organisation limits promotion and development prospects and so expanding into new territories creates the opportunity for staff to continue within the organisation. It also provides an experienced managerial resource to help transfer the organisation's experience into the new countries.

- **Accident** – some organisations have entered into overseas business literally without trying. Particularly recently, with the rise of the internet, it has been possible for potential customers to find an overseas supplier and make purchases without there having been any particular marketing activity or thought given to overseas sales. Whilst these unexpected sales can be sometimes seen as a little bonus there are significant issues related to the sales of products and services overseas that could create issues for even accidental sales or contracts. These really are not true international expansions but some of the legal and operational issues of international business will need to be taken into account.

6.2 Common issues for international expansion

With all overseas operations there are some common issues that face all models of expansion. These can be summarised as:

- **Local knowledge** – this is probably a bigger potential risk for a 100% owned direct investment but equally applies to some degree to all expansions. Although many staff will be hired locally there will always be the risk that the local market has not been fully understood in terms of product, pricing, competition, marketing, messaging and fulfilment. Should any of these fields be poorly managed then success may be limited.

- **Culture** – not only customer but also staff culture can be an issue with an overseas operation. Many countries operate a very hierarchical structure and local staff may be unwilling to make even minor decisions without managerial approval. Operating a division with either remote or imported managerial staff can cause substantial cultural issues within the organisation.

- **Distance** – it may seem obvious but remote operations will be at a distance. "Management by Walking About" is impossible. Communications will be much more formalised (even email is more formal than coffee machine chat). Staff in the remote organisation who have limited responsibility and no financial incentive for success may be reticent in communicating issues back to base. Issues may be left for far too long before rectification occurs.

- **Time** – even a one hour time difference can be an issue. With a normal 9–5 operation two hours per day may be lost due to either site being closed. Add in time for lunches (many European offices will still have formal one hour lunch breaks) and there will be limited time when both offices are synchronised. If the overseas operation is not fully autonomous, this can restrict its ability to operate effectively.

How these areas affect your business will need to be taken into account when planning your international operations.

6.3 Models for international expansion

The ways in which an organisation can manage its international operations are varied. With the exception of the accidental overseas seller any planned international expansion will take one of the following key forms:

Direct investment

This is the most explicit approach and probably offers both the highest risk and highest reward for international expansion. In this method, the business will endeavour to build a wholly owned subsidiary within the country. This subsidiary may be a duplicate image of the overall organisation with perhaps a global holding company overarching the various territorial organisations or it may rely to a great or lesser degree on the parent country to supply some centralised services.

For example the overseas organisation can be primarily a sales operation with virtually all manufacturing, research and development, accounting and finance operations taking place in the home country. Within this environment marketing may be limited to localising global campaigns and undertaking purely small scale localised activities with perhaps a market research activity to assist the central function with planning.

This minimal footprint operation may be most suitable within small territories and offers a relatively low cost means of entering a country whilst maximising returns to the organisation. However it very much relies on the overseas territory sharing many of the same attributes as the home country and assumes minimal localisation is required to meet the needs of the country.

In larger territories or where localisation is more clearly required then it is very likely that a wholesale transplant of many if not most functions would be required. This may also be a requirement within some territories which wish to ensure as much activity is internalised within the country. India is a particular example of this policy where the government, which has traditionally maintained a large degree of central control, often places significant constraints on organisations wishing to move into the region.

The use of direct investment as an expansion model of course maximises the percentage of the potential profit from the territory which is returned, but there are a number of issues with this approach:

- **Legal status** – the legal status of the overseas operation may generate substantial legal risks to the parent organisation. This Handbook is too short to cover all the potential risks but product liability (particularly in the USA) and general bankruptcy liabilities are of course the most obvious. By being 100% owned by the parent then not only is the financial liability 100% the responsibility of the parent but it is also impossible to spread the legal responsibility to local partners.

- **Leverage** – most oversees operations will require substantial investment and will operate in a cash-flow negative manner for a period of time. The costs of this will be borne by the parent, either directly from reserves or will need to be funded by loans supported by the home country cash flow. This could significantly increase the strain on the business as a whole and could both constrain local growth in the home market as well as expose the entire operation to risks.

The dilution of the direct investment by using local organisations to fund the business will enhance the business leverage of the expansion, reduce the cash flow strain and enable faster expansion.

- **Focus** – for many years the overseas operation will be generating little or no cash and yet will consume considerable management effort. There is a danger that the focus will either be taken away from the core home business or that the "trivial" overseas operation will be starved of time and/or resources. With the two operations at different phases it is sometimes possible to direct the correct resources to both but it is extremely difficult to provide the same level of managerial focus on both operations at the same time.

Joint ventures

It is for these reasons that most organisations will (at least for the first territory) consider some form of joint venture. These JVs can take many forms:

- Agents
- Distributors
- Partnerships

Agents

This is the lowest cost method of entering a market. An overseas agent works in a similar manner to an in country agent. They will usually be single person or very small businesses offering their services as an independent sales person. Almost invariably they will represent multiple organisations and will usually only be paid on a commission basis. Many will undertake some aspects of the import activities (ensuring customs policies are followed, etc.), and a few will undertake local invoicing – remitting monies (minus their commission and any local taxes) back to the home country. In regions where import duties are complex and currency is tightly controlled these functions can be of significant benefit to an organisation.

An agent will normally not hold substantial stocks (except in the case of high volume, low value items).

Within a marketing function, this type of operation can have pros and cons:

Pros

- The agent will be independent and will almost certainly have their own CRM systems/contacts
- Lead generation will not be expected beyond forwarding any web-based leads or speculative queries

Cons

- The agent will be working for many companies and so marketing and branding can be very diluted (Formula 1 car syndrome) with multiple competing brands being offered
- Marketing materials may need to be centrally produced or, if the production is outsourced, quality control may be required to ensure marketing and branding rules are maintained.
- The agent will have extremely low commitment to any single brand and will be happy to offer whatever brands he feels will make the sale to the customer quickly
- There is the risk of commission inflation and/or price erosion to attempt to ensure the agent offers your product in preference to others. Both reduce net income and will need control

> Formula 1 is an extremely expensive sport and the competitors require $10 million of sponsorship every year to compete effectively. As few organisations are large enough to support this level of sponsorship individually, the teams will frequently have a large number of sponsors each paying a different level of sponsorship for differing amounts of coverage. Most of this coverage is in the form of sponsor logos on the cars and the overalls of drivers. Therefore frequently the cars will have the logos of 10–20 different companies. Drivers may also have personal sponsors resulting in their overalls having even more logos. It is noticeable that one of the first things a F1 driver will do before a post-race interview is to put on the sponsors baseball cap to ensure their logo is visible!

Other business issues may include:

- **Presence** – if a competitor has a more substantial presence in the region, your company could be seen as being less committed to the region and so major contracts may be difficult to gain.

- **Pre and after-sales support** – an agent is unlikely to have a substantial pre-sales or after-sales support function and so products that require significant pre-sales work (consultative selling, design, etc.) may be unobtainable or require head office involvement. This either reduces potential sales or increases costs of sales. After-sales support is likely to be hard to offer through an agency model (which typically does not carry spares or replacement items).

- **Limited resources, limited ambitions** – an agent may have limited means to deal with all the potential customers. If they can make a good living on 10% of $2,000,000 aggregated sales from all their lines and they have five ranges, your company's share of that $2,000,000 may be relatively small. The agent will have little incentive to expand and so the overseas operation may never generate a substantial return.

For this reason agencies are largely used in countries where tactical rather than strategic expansion is considered.

An agent may have a very limited geographical spread and so it may be possible to operate numerous agents within a territory provided clear lines of responsibility and conflict resolution are created.

Distributors
A distributor within a country may have a notionally similar structure to an agent but will typically be larger enterprises with more substantial pre-sales support, internal marketing functions, warehousing and physical distribution facilities (where appropriate) and some after-sales support functions. To many intents they may be considered to be very

much more self-sufficient as companies with the main company acting more as a manufacturing function to the distributor sales channel.

Again many will be multi-product distributors this is the norm with very few independent distributors handling only one line (the motor industry being a notable exception where single product distributors are relatively common).

Distributors tend to be much more self-sufficient and arguably professional and so many of the issues relating to agents no longer apply or apply to a lesser extent. However the issues of multi-product conflict and cannibalisation will still occur and need to be pro-actively managed.

Within the distributor channel the marketing role will largely be responsible for:

- Co-ordination of any global campaigns
- Training
- Core material production for localisation
- Monitoring of locally produced content for compliance and brand consistency

In some respects a distributor, with a more substantial marketing function, may impose at least different, and in some cases greater, demands on the central marketing function. They may be more demanding for bespoke content, may be more likely to create their own content if central content is not available and may be more likely to engage in 'brand drift'.

One typical answer to many of these issues is the creation of firm brand standards and to provide substantial core materials which can be localised easily. This may create a substantial front-loading of the marketing effort but this can be reused in many territories and it is often found that most organisations will take the path of least resistance and will follow standards and templates that have been created in preference to creating their own.

At this point the distributor is still an independent organisation with its own business goals and strategies. This means that these goals and strategies may not completely coincide with those of your organisation, or if they do, may not always coincide. As a result, many organisations will either develop a partnership with a distributor or set up a partnership from scratch.

Partnerships
At the partnership stage the level of direct investment from the parent company increases rapidly. A significant proportion of the start-up costs and running costs of the partnership will be borne by the parent with the remainder covered by the local partner.

The local partner may take a number of forms ranging from simply a source of local funding and knowledge to a near equal industry wanting to combine the range of products and services. In some countries the government will select a local partner as a requirement for granting a licence.

Partnerships are configured as separate legal entities and remit income back to the parent company in a number of forms. Firstly relationships between the parent and the partnership will be contractual with pricing for goods and services. Services can include management, consultancy, marketing support, Intellectual Property Rights (IPR) licences and products. These services form a method of withdrawing cash from the local business and the local economy and so need to be managed to ensure any legal requirements within the local business regulations are upheld.

Removing monies in this way has the effect of reducing the net profits of the local organisation. The local partner will also consider these to be part of the return on investment made by the parent and so the split in profits (in the form of dividends) will need to be adjusted to ensure total profits from the local business are divided in proportion to the investments placed.

From a marketing perspective there will be substantially more control over the business than in either agency or distributor models. In fact the business is likely to be a sole product partnership and so will act much more like a remote division with a larger proportion of some functions centralised (in particular marketing). This in itself creates greater challenges to the marketing function. This could be because the level of local knowledge within the central function may be relatively limited. The organisation may also decide to minimise costs by relying on the 'head office' marketing functions and undertaking only minimal localisation of marketing content. Examples of this can readily be seen with poor quality, badly dubbed TV adverts or localised material being badly edited into a stock advert.

In many companies the head office will attempt to minimise local taxation by charging remote divisions high fees for 'marketing support'. The use of these funding mechanisms to 'return' marketing functions and funds to the home country may exacerbate this problem as there are both limited funds remaining and the desire to make full use of the central materials which have been expensively purchased!

Even with a separate legal entity in place, in order to reduce the costs (and maximise return) many functions will run with skeleton staff in the country with management undertaken remotely and only relatively junior staff local. This can again cause cultural problems. In many countries and regions (Southern Europe, Asia, Middle and Far East) management will be expected to undertake virtually all decision making with staff merely acting as multiple, remote hands to 'do management's bidding'.

This runs counter to the 'empowerment' culture that occurs in many other countries. In the absence of frequent and active control it is very easy for staff not used to empowerment to freeze and make only limited decisions without managerial approval. Although some basic functions of marketing are not dramatically affected by this issue (though the extra delay involved in micro-management needs to be considered), other more strategic functions that rely on both local awareness and self-motivation (market research, opportunity scanning, media selection etc.) will need careful management and coordination at a level the central office may not be used to undertaking.

In summary all these models of international business distribution offer different challenges and opportunities and impose different (though related) challenges within the marketing spectrum.

As can be seen there is a natural progression from Agent through Distributors, and Partnerships to Fully Owned Subsidiaries and as this changes so does the role of marketing.

In many large multi-nationals all these models may exist simultaneously with agents breaking new ground then followed by distributors before 'on-the-ground' investments take place. In this circumstance it may be that the marketing role has to take different functions simultaneously to support the different simultaneous distribution modes.

6.4 Brand and IPR protection

Brand and IPR protection is an area within marketing that is extremely broad and, particularly within the IPR arena, requires substantial legal expertise. This Handbook cannot offer any more than initial pointers to the issues of brand and IPR within an international field. Any organisation planning any more than the barest minimum of overseas activity should seek expert advice from an organisation experienced in the legal framework of the countries where you plan to operate. Many organisations will have substantial legal teams retained solely to manage brands and IPR and these will often be selected from a law firm which specialises in this arena rather than from the usual firm or in-house team.

Some areas of International Branding and IPR that will be of interest to the marketing function can be summarised as follows:

Trademarks

Trademarks are the usual protection mechanism for brands and logos. Trademarks are usually registered within each country though some trademark registrations can cover multiple countries (particularly within

Europe). The registering of trademarks in each country (particularly when covering all variants and categories) can be an expensive activity. The temptation can be to delay registering trademarks if it is uncertain if trading will take place within a territory – this can be false economy as many countries have a very lax attitude towards branding and trademarks. The lack of a trademark in a country will tempt local businesses to try to sell on the back of an established brand – usually with inferior products or service. This can damage the brand reputation of your business before you have entered the territory making later entry into the region difficult.

Although registering a trademark within a territory will not prevent this activity it can make it easier to enforce action against local businesses as most countries are now willing to take action if there is a clear legal requirement to do so.

One of the most copied and abused trademarks in the world is Coca-Cola with virtually every East European, African, South American and Asian Country having multiple products attempting to pass themselves off as the original. Many of these products are made in back-street operations in virtually 'pop-up' factories. The capabilities of digital printing technologies make it possible for these products to produce convincing facsimiles of logos and branding. For many products much work is undertaken to make the packaging very expensive to reproduce (complex shapes to bottles, cans, etc.). This both reduces the incentive to duplicate products and makes it easier for consumers to identify fakes.

Patents
With a Patent it is necessary to reveal details of how your product is made and its functions. Consequently other organisations become aware of the details of your product. In an international sense this can be an issue because it would allow companies in countries not covered by your patent to copy your products.

In order to ensure patents protect your business overseas most countries use the Patent Co-operation Treaty to simplify the filing of patents, ensure patent priority is given, and reduce the initial search fees (local registration fees still apply). The UK is party to the Patent Co-operation Treaty (PCT). Under the PCT you can file a single international patent application with a PCT Receiving Office in one language and in accordance with one set of rules, seeking simultaneous patent protection in a number of PCT contracting States.

Design rights

Design rights are in some cases similar to both patents and trademarks as they deal with the physical appearance of the product as well as some operational characteristics (placement of buttons, controls etc.). For a product where the physical appearance is a crucial aspect of the product and there is a desire to reduce the likelihood of copying, then registering for Registered Design Rights should be considered. Design Rights are relatively limited and cannot be relied upon to protect products.

Copyright

Copyright protects written, musical and artistic works as well as film, book layouts, sound recordings, and broadcasts. Copyright is an 'automatic right', which means you do not have to apply for it. It is not necessary to 'claim' copyright within any creative product (book, film, etc.) though this usually is done to assert the authorship and date of copyright as this can make any legal actions easier to undertake. It has limited applicability to most products and services.

Marketing implications

The overall marketing implications of IPR within an international sphere are in general similar to those within the national space. However application and enforcement of IPR can vary from territory to territory and so it is necessary to ensure that both your brands and trademarks are protected to the fullest extent.

Other implications may revolve around your adverts. Music may be under a different copyright holder and so permission may need to be sought. Slogans and other marks may be trademarked differently and may need to be adjusted or permission sought from the local owners.

For more information on IPR and its general implications within your business it is recommended that independent expert advice is sought.

6.5 International culture

The local culture of a new territory is a vital consideration for the marketing mix. This is more than just language but involves the entire communication method.

Some countries have a much slower pace of negotiation for contracts. Friendship, trust and relationships are often valued more highly in the Middle East than the final price of the service. In these areas frequently changing account managers (a common practice in Western Europe) is frowned upon and buyers will often move their business to follow a friend rather than accept new relationships.

Email and telephone contact is commonplace in many countries but in parts of the world only face-to-face communication is considered suitable and companies who try to impose 'outsider' business practices will be unsuccessful.

As an example a large telecoms company wanted to close a contract in Jordan. In Europe, this contract would have normally taken 2–3 people one week conducted mainly by phone, email and video conferencing. In Jordan all three were invited to stay at the customer's expense for nearly three weeks, much of which was spent meeting a variety of interested parties who needed to be 'involved' in the decision.

Sexual equality can affect the sales and marketing mix. In many countries buyers will prefer to deal with a more junior man than the more senior woman. Adverts which show men in a 'lesser' role to women will not be effective. Of course sexually charged adverts can be a major issue.

One example of the issues of sexual equality occurred within the motor industry. The overseas sales department of a luxury car manufacturer employed a mixture of men and women. When calls came in from the Middle Eastern distributors any woman answering the phone would be faced with silence and a rapidly disconnected call due to the male owner of the distributor refusing to speak to a woman.

Many major companies have fallen foul of the issues of culture within a new country but some have made 'too much effort' and this has been equally counter-productive. There are many examples of organisations 're-colouring' actors in adverts to suit different markets – this crude refocusing can backfire and the companies can be seen as pandering to racial or sexual discrimination. In these cases it can be worth creating completely new adverts locally through agencies that understand the issues of culture and to avoid direct comparison with adverts in other countries.

Chapter 7: Services Distribution

Marketing services through a distribution model has an extremely long and varied history. In fact most consumer financial services prior to widespread personal bank accounts were managed through door-to-door agents selling insurance and collecting premiums directly from the householder. This model still widely existed in the UK until the late 1980s and a rump of this still exists even now though focused on lower socio-economic groups.

With the advance of phone and on-line sales and marketing activities there are still two main distribution models used for services marketing: direct and indirect.

7.1 Direct marketing

Direct marketing of services is often seen as the easiest, cheapest and most cost-effective distribution method as it reduces the distance between the provider and consumer. The nature of services means that physical distribution is not required (even the distribution of documentation can be conducted on-line). The self-service nature of the internet allows the centralised costs of staff and support to be minimised.

The removal of intermediaries also reduces the transaction costs for services – in the UK 40% of all car tax discs (the annual 'road fund' tax imposed by government) are now sold on-line reducing both the administrative overhead and the fees paid to the post office (which sells the remainder).

It is the prospect of reducing these processing and transaction costs that is the primary driver for much centralisation. The lower level of costs can either be used to reduce prices/fees for services, or increase profit margin and return on investment. In many cases the reduction in costs can turn a marginal business model into a profitable one.

One of the primary issues with direct services distribution (particularly centralised delivery models) is the customer relationship management and marketing activity.

Services, by definition, have no physical product. The consumer is getting little or nothing visible for their money. There is therefore little incentive to buy services unless they are essential or compulsory (banking, insurance, or tax discs). This means that the seller of these services has to undertake substantial demand generation activities. This demand generation is in two forms:

- **New service sales** – this is an attempt to sell a new, previously unknown service to a customer base
- **Switching sales** – an attempt to persuade a customer to move from one service provider to another

New service sales

Marketing a brand new, previously unknown, service to an audience is a lengthy and complex process. It requires a substantial level of user education regarding not only the service but also the need for the service.

As a service provider you will have identified a gap in the market that your service fills. However, your target customers may not be aware of this gap. You will need therefore to educate your audience and demonstrate to them the need for the service. This is merely the first task. Once the potential customers have been educated they need to select you as the supplier of that service.

If you do not have an existing customer relationship with them then the process of educating a user about the need for a product is extremely difficult. If the customer does not know they need a service and does not know such a service exists s/he should they look for a service. This issue is frequently known as 'a solution in search of a problem'.

The only solution to this within the direct distribution model is via comprehensive advertising and awareness marketing.

The problem with attempting to raise awareness of a problem through advertising is, quite simply, the ability to capture the attention of the audience for long enough to read/listen to the explanation of the problem then continue to understand the solution you are offering. This is an extremely information dense process and one which takes substantial investment in time and resources.

It is hard to identify an example of a new service that has been successfully introduced recently outside the on-line sphere and in most of those cases (Hotmail, iTunes, Dropbox, etc.) they have been mainly limited to on-line variations of existing products and services and so are not primarily new services. On-line service distribution will be discussed later in this Handbook but largely relies on low take-up rates within huge populations followed by viral (self) marketing. This process can succeed within the on-line sphere but is hard to justify within the more traditional service marketing opportunities.

Switch sales

Because it is extremely difficult and expensive to introduce a genuinely new service (particularly through a direct model) most direct service organisations focus on switch selling to persuade users of competitor services to move to a new provider. This is of particular relevance to services that are annual or annually renewed (insurance in particular). These services can see switching rates in excess of 30% per year (Onlyinsurance.com, n.d) in the UK. This process is termed 'churn'.

Service providers seek to reduce this churn through a variety of means. The first is, of course, automatic renewal "You don't need to do anything, your insurance will be renewed automatically". This is usually accompanied by the new price but no information on the previous price of the service. This checking is left to the buyer who is then faced with undertaking a number of activities himself before making an active decision to move. Churn reduction is usually undertaken by making passivity the default choice for the consumer. By not checking and by not changing, the service will continue. This relies on the inertia of the consumer. The increasing use of direct bank transfer to pay bills has also reduced churn (a factor which is behind much of the push of service providers to use this payment method).

Inertia within annually renewed services is still high (a churn of 30% still leaves a retention rate of 70%) but within services that do not renew, churn can be extremely low. For example annual churn rates for bank accounts can be as low as 2–3% with 38% of customers never having changed bank in their lifetime (Smith, 2012). A large factor in this inertia is the perceived complications in switching services. This is compounded by the preponderance of direct debit payments used by customers – the chance that one of the many direct debit payments will fail is considered to be a major factor in the reluctance to change bank accounts. In an increasingly electronic financial market, switching banking provider can be seen as being as risky as performing a major service on your car whilst driving along the motorway!

Other services (such as mobile phones, broadband, etc.) impose significant financial penalties for early switching and many will offer free upgrades and/or discounts just before renewal time to lock the customer into a new long-term contract.

Defensive positions like these are typical within mature markets where there is little opportunity to grow the absolute size of the market and so market share capture is the principle source of growth. Within some markets (e.g. mobile phones) there is still some opportunity for absolute growth (particularly by targeting younger users), but within other markets (e.g energy supply) the opportunity for growth is extremely limited and so churn is the only growth strategy available.

Within this competitive market the marketing of switch selling to consumers is a difficult activity best likened to WW1 trench warfare with both sides fighting hard to retain customers. Within mature markets this becomes a zero sum game.

Other factors also apply. Although the notional entry cost for a new entrant into a mature service market is low (due to low cap-ex costs and the lack of a distribution channel which requires investment to grow), established suppliers have in-built advantages. Even with churn of 30% this still leaves a rump of 70% of clients who offer a consistent revenue source at rates that, on aggregate, are likely to be higher than the current baseline market rate. In contrast, the company entering the market has no 'rump' of customers on more expensive contracts and so its average income per customer is much lower. The new entrant therefore has to fund client acquisition through aggressive pricing whilst not having an established customer base with which to cross-subsidise it. An established provider also has this revenue base with which to fund its marketing activities.

One organisation which has managed to succeed in entering service industries has been the Virgin Group. In this case the organisation has benefited from a number of advantages. Firstly, being a group of companies it has reserves to enable it to fund initially loss-making entry strategies at low cost. Secondly it has an established brand (centred around its founder) which enables rapid brand recognition even within markets where it has not previously competed. Finally the majority of its entrances into new markets have been on the back of acquisitions and/or mergers with established players (Virgin Media/NTL, Virgin Bank/Northern Rock) which have brought expertise and an established customer base.

Churn reduction through new service delivery

One of the most common and effective means of churn reduction is the cross-selling of services to existing customers. Depending on the industry and the products this can reduce churn by between 30% and 80%. The most effective strategy is to offer existing customers new and 'unique' services in conjunction with their existing service offering. This of course has three main effects:

- First, churn is reduced.
- Second, additional income is generated from existing customers.
- Thirdly, the targeted marketing of a service to existing customers is, in general, easier, cheaper and quicker than more mass-market promotion. These customers already know the organisation, have some degree of trust in the company and are known to be using related products. Conversion rates within this group are therefore likely to be higher than in the general population.

As a result of this, whilst a direct distribution model within service industries offers significant opportunities, both the delivery of new services and the marketing of existing services offer considerable challenges to the marketing function. The services industries therefore tend towards oligopoly structures with large established players competing in a near zero-sum game environment.

The other approach for sales of service products is via an indirect channel.

7.2 Indirect marketing

Owing to the difficulty in entering the services sector using a direct selling approach, many new entrants will opt for an indirect model using an intermediary to sell those services.

Typical intermediary mechanisms include:

- Independent advisors (primarily Independent Financial Advisors (IFAs))
- Comparison sites (available for the majority of services)
- Independent retail sites (mainly within the mobile phone/device market)

The role of IFAs within the financial services sector has recently been problematic with concerns over miss-selling (recommending products based on commissions earned rather than the suitability of the product) or in many cases fraud (particularly collusion in the self-certified mortgage market). However they do have a significant role to play within the medium to high value client base where tax and retirement planning benefit from their ability to assess the various options available to clients and select the ones best suited to them. Marketing to IFAs requires the ability to communicate complex information rapidly and effectively. (New regulations came into force in January 2013 preventing the direct or indirect payment of IFAs by supplying organisations. This is an attempt to ensure that advice is separated from any potential fees earned by the IFA to ensure neutrality.) The laws and regulations surrounding marketing to IFAs are complex and specific to both the products and the market and so expert legal advice is recommended to assess any marketing activities in this field.

Whereas IFAs have a distinct role within the medium to high value market for financial services where a personal approach and highly specialist knowledge is key, this level of personal interaction within the lower vale 'commodity' services is not sustainable. This has led to a huge growth in the market for comparison sites. Within the UK the main players are:

- www.moneysupermarket.com
- www.Comparethemarket.com
- www.Gocompare.com
- www.fool.co.uk
- www.uswitch.com
- www.moneynet.co.uk
- www.moneyexpert.com
- www.moneyextra.com
- www.moneyfacts.co.uk
- www.kelkoo.co.uk

These sites earn referral fees from the providers of the services. For the majority of the services offered, lowest price tends to be the primary buying factor and this coupled with the requirement to pay the referral fee can lead to the suppliers focusing on extremely low margin business. This business is also likely to be relatively high churn (as it was captured through an intermediary it is probable that the customer will use the same comparison site in the future). Customer loyalty tends to be with the comparison site rather than with the supplier.

This source of business may be attractive to many of the smaller service providers (it is notable that many of the best deals tend to be from much smaller organisations) as it gives them equal visibility compared to the more established brands. It is the combination of low margin, high threat of churn and the threat of comparison with smaller organisations that has persuaded many larger service providers not to take part in these sites.

The comparison sites began with insurance products (usually because these are annually renewed services and so there is a consistent flow of new business opportunities), but have rapidly moved into virtually every service sector including utilities, financial services (credit cards and personal bank accounts particularly) and even mobile phone and broadband services. This market has been growing at an annualised rate of at least 30% for the past 4–5 years (Wood, 2007).

The other significant arena of third party service sales is within the independent mobile phone market (principally Phones 4u and Carphone Warehouse in the UK). Although notionally product sales, the core income from these products arises from the monthly contract fees and so should really be considered to be a service rather than product sale. It is the on-going revenues from each sale that maintains these as viable businesses. The overall business and marketing structure of the mobile phone industry (Dedrick et al, 2010) is a hugely complex field of its own and is beyond the scope of this Handbook.

Within this section analysis, has shown the effects that on-line distribution models have had in the service marketing sector. The on-line environment has led to a huge variety of opportunities for both existing and new business models.

Chapter 8: Electronic Distribution Models
8.1 The internet

2012 saw the 20th anniversary of the first image to be uploaded to the internet (Poeter, 2012). In those 20 years the internet has hugely affected virtually every aspect of business life. Many thousands of businesses have been created to support the on-line marketplace, thousands more to exploit the opportunities offered and there are an equal number of established businesses who have seen their traditional markets damaged by new entrants and new opportunities from the internet.

At its most basic level, the internet offers many organisations another route to market for their current products or services. This is typified by organisations such as Direct Line (which offered a phone-based insurance and mortgage service) simply using the internet as a second shop front for their existing products, or Next who had an established mail order catalogue business and now use the internet to largely supersede the catalogue sales. For each of these organisations the changes were relatively simple – they both had business models and processes set up for remote distribution and so the transition to on-line marketing, sales and fulfilment was relatively painless. Other organisation types have had different experiences.

Financial services and the internet

Financial services companies (primarily banks) have been able to migrate a very substantial level of their basic transactional business to an on-line model reducing the workloads within branches to those activities that require face-to-face interaction (cash handling etc.) and freeing staff to perform more sales focused roles. This second role is in many ways a double edged sword. With staff being more focused on selling new services and significant push-back from customers to this hard sell approach, those customers who can avoid branch visits do so leaving the branches to support a decreasing rump of customers who, through their profile, are less likely to be able to purchase extra services.

This trend for many customers to eschew branch banking will probably continue and accelerate – though interestingly on-line only banks (such as Smile) still have a very small market share (between 2% and 5% of the marketing depending on the product (House of Commons Treasury Committee, 2011)). This indicates that either customers prefer having a physical branch network as an option or that the provision of on-line banking services has helped traditional banks fight against the churn on which the on-line providers were relying.

Interestingly business banking services tend to use a more balanced mix of on-line and physical branch banking. This tends to be as a result of the need for cash handling (the vast majority of small and medium businesses will undertake some form of cash handling and the number of these businesses is much greater than other business size categories), and also to provide access to business advisors able to provide support for the wider variety of business focused services.

High street retail
Of the business groups that have found it hardest to adapt to the on-line business models it has been high street retail that has suffered the most. The main issues have been twofold.

Firstly, on-line retailing has, in general, lower overheads than high street business (warehouse and distribution centres are in general cheaper than high street stores and, in any case, are equally needed by a large retail chain). This reduces the entry cost for competitors who do not need to fund a large scale retail distribution network.

Secondly, a high street business finds it difficult to offer lower prices through its on-line channel, otherwise much of the sales gained will be cannibalised from high street customers. This reduces their competitiveness in the on-line space at the same time as on-line competitors are affecting their high street sales.

Some sectors have been extremely hard hit – particularly books (by Amazon and increasingly e-books), and Music and DVD (by services such as iTunes and, in the DVD arena, companies such as LoveFilm and Netflix). These sectors which focus on the sale of content are seeing massively rapid changes. Whereas Amazon started (and is still strong) in the on-line sale and then physical delivery of books and DVDs, many new entrants are focusing on a 100% on-line sale and delivery model with no physical product ever being produced. Other sectors which have been affected (albeit to a slightly lesser extent) have been the electronics and 'brown goods' sectors. This has been a result of a combination of the buyer profile (largely male aged 20–40) which fits closely with the early penetration of the internet and the increase in review and comparison sites for equipment that then allow purchases from sponsoring retailers.

Other sectors have been less badly affected – particularly clothing. This is partially down to the customer profile (in the early days of on-line marketing) but can be largely attributed to the nature of the product where look, feel, quality and most importantly, fit play a major role in the buying process and cannot easily be replicated on-line. In 2011 it was estimated that 33% of on-line clothing sales were returned costing retailers £100 million in postage and spoilage (Skrill, 2011). Non-standard sizing was estimated to be the biggest reason behind returns. This may go some way to explain why of the top 50 on-line retailers in the UK in 2011 only 7 sold clothing (NetImperative, 2011).

Areas which have been a success have been men's clothing (which tends to be a less fashion conscious field and has more consistent sizing) and lingerie (where sizing is slightly more consistent).

New business opportunities

The internet has offered many organisations the opportunity to create business models that would otherwise not be possible. This can either be businesses that are purely on-line based (such as Social Media businesses, Cloud computing software services, audio and video streaming or downloading) or businesses for which a physical operation would not be cost effective or profitable. Within the second group are many specialist retailers or service providers for whom the density of potential customers is too low to justify physical premises or distribution within any region and the marketing of the services would be too expensive to reach. The internet allows these businesses to create a worldwide presence without the costs normally associated with building a nationwide or worldwide distribution platform.

Within these business types the marketing has to reflect the products and services offered. If the services are very specialist then mass marketing is clearly not appropriate. If the services/products are new and market education/creation is key then simple SEO and PPC advertising is unlikely to be the principal route (put simply if no-one knows about your product, who is going to search for it!).Consequently a targeted education/information strategy is important. If the product/service is well known within the user community then 'traditional' SEO and PPC marketing may be the best route to gain market share.

Hybrid models

An alternative structure that has been successful for many smaller high street retailers has been a hybrid model where an on-line operation has been used to supply demand in those regions where there is insufficient density to support physical distribution. Operations such as Pandora, Swarovski and Links of London have simultaneously developed both a physical distribution and an on-line presence. This allows these businesses to leverage more large scale marketing activities knowing that those potential customers not near a physical site will still be able to respond to the call to action. It is notable that this strategy tends to be employed by higher end organisations where the purchasing process is part of the 'retail experience'. This retail experience/gratification element provides a value add within the store that is harder to replicate on-line and so justifies both channels operating.

Brand strategy and the internet

One of the biggest problems that the internet poses for marketing is maintaining the brand. Because the internet offers an extremely low cost of entry for businesses, and the creation of an on-line brand does not require major investment in premises or physical advertising, it is very hard to maintain strong brand values when competing alongside on-line brands. This is a particular issue when selling branded goods through a third party distribution channel.

8.2 On-line selling and the influence of eBay and Amazon

The on-line Ecommerce market has grown year on year and now accounts for 17% of the UK retail market. As a result many retailers have recently opted to investigate selling products on-line.

Many established brands have been able to transfer their physical brands across to the internet, and many have built a presence solely on-line. Of these the two largest are, of course, eBay and Amazon.

Both of these brands started with a very specific target market (second-hand personal items and books respectively) and have branched out into many other areas, in particular, acting as distribution channels for other organisations.

eBay

eBay was at the vanguard (accidentally) of the approach of business selling with the creation of a vast number of professional and semi-professional business sellers offering large ranges of brand-new items (mainly sold for fixed prices). Many major brands now use eBay to sell returned items or clearance items. These very large brands see the use of eBay as a useful way to hide these returns and clearance lines and to use the cover of eBay to disguise the sales and protect their main brand. This technique allows them to reduce the dilution of their primary brand through a channel.

Alongside these major brands are many thousands of small, medium and very small businesses (often home businesses) selling through eBay and attempting to build on-line retail enterprises. These small on-line sellers are using the eBay brand and its extremely wide coverage to leverage sales. The costs of setting up a dedicated on-line store are relatively low in comparison to a physical Bricks and Mortar (B&M) store but the costs (in time and money) of ensuring high search engine placement and sufficient sales can be extremely high and so eBay can be seen as a quick and easy channel to sales.

This market entry strategy (using eBay as a low entry cost distribution channel then moving to an external channel) is unfortunately rarely successful for the following reasons:

- Competitors on eBay can never be effectively driven out of the market as there is a continual stream of new entrants each hoping to take control of the market. The low cost of entry (Porter, 2008) means that it is impossible to gain control of the distribution channel. (There will always be a newcomer who believes they can make a fortune by undercutting the opposition).

- Buyers on eBay are purchasing from eBay. In many cases they will barely register the identity of the seller they are using. If the process is a success then they will communicate with their peers on the success of their eBay purchase. Only if it is a failure will they recognise or remember the identity of the seller. The level of brand loyalty to a particular seller is tiny with most brand loyalty retained by eBay.

It is sometimes possible for an eBay seller to convert eBay buyers into direct channel buyers but this often requires further discounts compared to sale prices on eBay and is a time consuming and expensive process. The buyer has already demonstrated a preference for buying via eBay and so this buying pattern must be broken.

Buying and by inference selling through eBay is considered a 'budget' affair. People looking for bargains look to eBay and so there is a significant danger that brands seen on eBay are seen as budget.

This is a particular issue when an organisation is offering its products through multiple channels (particularly non on-line) as well as eBay as buyers will both look to use eBay to find lower prices (affecting the sales and profitability of other sellers) and also consider the brand to be less exclusive because of its availability via eBay.

Amazon

Amazon has also developed a distribution channel offering for third parties. In this case the channel is more closely aligned with business sellers (there are stringent qualification criteria for many categories), only fixed price selling is permitted, the use of the Amazon payment gateway is compulsory and, uniquely, Amazon has a warehousing, packaging and fulfilment offering to enable this element of the value chain to be completely outsourced.

In the case of businesses selling through Amazon the issues related to eBay still exist, and in many cases are exacerbated, but further constraints also apply:

- Due to the listing mechanism within Amazon each UPC (equivalent to the product barcode) is listed only once with each seller of that product acting as a competing supplier for that product. There is also virtually no branding that can be applied by the seller on their product listing which is shared (including photos) with all other sellers of the same UPC coded item. This results in price being the primary differentiator between sellers. Only in the cases where substantial differences in service and/or customer care exist will there be any impetus to select a higher priced offer. There are also tools that allow automatic undercutting of competitor prices so a vicious spiral of price cutting can occur. Coupled with the (generally) higher sales fees there is a real risk of selling for negative margin using this business model.

- The 'fulfilment by Amazon' option offers businesses a very quick and simple approach to retail sales but unless margins are very closely monitored this system can also result in negative margins.

- Finally and most importantly, selling through Amazon gives Amazon direct sales data on your product sales and average selling price. Amazon can then use this sales data to decide if the products have sufficient demand to justify their own stocks.

In effect Amazon is being paid by companies to sell their products whilst those companies carry out market research for Amazon. There have been numerous examples of new lines being sold on Amazon so successfully that Amazon has then gone on to stock those lines at reduced prices (owing to a combination of buying power and reduced costs).

In neither of these cases do the sellers have significant opportunities to build their own brand. They are essentially stocking the shelves of eBay and Amazon (and to a limited extent other similar organisations) and offering these companies virtually zero risk revenue streams. Because the cost of entry into this channel has been set so low there is always a significant pipeline of new entrants to the market which maintains price competitiveness and ensures that no single seller gains any degree of control over the sales channel.

Interestingly they have opted to focus on slightly different product profiles. eBay tends to focus on cheap, low end, low price, unbranded items or branded catalogue items at substantially below recommended retail price (rrp). Amazon tends to focus on branded items with prices set in comparison to rrp and is almost exclusively used to sell new items.

The power of these two brands (eBay and Amazon) is such that they rarely need to undertake much marketing activity. They have such control over this marketplace that many buyers will bypass searching and go directly through eBay or Amazon.

Within both of these channels the brand of the products sold has become almost secondary to the brand of the two sellers. (During the production of this handbook Play.com an on-line retailer which initially focused on music and DVDs announced the cessation of its direct shipment model (where it purchased, stocked and distributed goods) to focus entirely on acting as a marketplace for other sellers. This dramatically demonstrates the power of this marketplace model.)

The effect of eBay and Amazon on B2C on-line sales

This dominance has had a dramatic effect on the structure of the B2C on-line sales channels. Organisations hoping to sell ranges of relatively generic items find themselves competing against two immensely strong retail brands that have become the default search engines within this channel. Only when buyers cannot find the required products within eBay or Amazon are other channels investigated.

In order for an on-line sales channel to be effective within this virtual oligopoly there has to be substantial value added by the retailer to override the market dominance of these aggregated sellers. During the production of this Handbook, Play.com, an on-line retailer which initially focused on music and DVDs, announced the cessation of its direct shipment model (where it purchased, stocked and distributed goods) to focus entirely on acting as a marketplace for other sellers. This dramatically demonstrates the power of this marketplace model.

A number of factors can generate this added value:

- **Exclusivity** – many brands (particularly high-end brands) are refusing to provide stock to sellers wishing to offer products via (particularly) eBay
- **Customisation** – there are significant limitations on the ability to sell customised items on these platforms – particularly Amazon which requires individual UPCs for each item sold
- **Specialisation** – some products benefit from specialised retail channels that can offer a range of advice, support and skills that are unachievable through generic sales portals

In summary it is vital to understand the risks and opportunities offered by channels such as eBay and Amazon. These channels offer established brands an opportunity to sell through overstocks, returns and experimental or opportunistic lines at relatively low cost and without risking damaging the original brand. However as an initial step in a brand creation strategy or as the sole sales channel they expose the organisation to potentially significant revenue costs whilst not providing a long term sustainable brand development strategy.

8.3 Disintermediation via online distribution

Within the services section of this Handbook we discussed how on-line delivery has enabled organisations to remove layers of distribution and so improve margins and control of the market. Within the physical product arena there is an equal opportunity/temptation to undertake the same process. The question is simple 'Why should I sell to a retailer at 50% of rrp when I can set up a simple website and sell direct to the consumer at rrp?' (A manufacturer will typically sell to its retailers at approximately 50% of the recommended retail price – so an item for sale in the high street at £10 was typically purchased by the retailer for £5. The manufacturer makes a relatively small margin on the £5 trade price. The retailer has the remainder of the margin to cover all selling costs of the product.) Whilst the question is simple the answer is usually less than clear.

Throughout this handbook the concept of value adding through the distribution channel has been discussed. Each step through the channel adds a particular value and so removing that step requires that this value is re-added at some other point.

In many cases the value that the retailer is adding to the product is, simply, other products. A manufacturer of batteries could consider a separate on-line retail site but the majority of battery sales are in conjunction with a battery powered item or are impulse/forced purchases at a physical point of sale within a shop. Batteries are not normally an item the typical buyer will consider as a primary purchase and so the opportunity for disintermediation is reduced.

A good example of how an attempted disintermediation failed was with a toy distributor in the UK. This distributor sold a wide range of cheap, pocket money toys primarily to the small independent toy stores across the UK. The typical retail price of these toys was in the range of £2–£4 (trade price £1–£2). The toys were targeted as pocket money items or 'stocking fillers' and were often purchased for 'party bags' for children's parties.

The distributor identified an opportunity to bypass its sales base and to set up both physical stores and an on-line presence to sell exactly the same items at the rrp that its buyers were selling for and so internalise that profit.

The key problems with this strategy were twofold:

- First the items were 'pocket money' items purchased literally with pocket money by children and on impulse. This is completely different to an on-line model which requires a credit or debit card (not normally available to under 18s) and incurs postage charges which given the typical value of the sale were a significant proportion of the total basket value.
- Secondly these items were normally co-located with other higher value items in the toyshop (or at the till point). Therefore the parental buyer would add these little items to their overall purchase 'as a treat'. They were not the primary reason for entering the store. Even the party bag market did not offer sufficient sales because again the toy store could add extra value in the form of bags, sweets etc. that the distributors website did not carry.

Even within their own branded stores success was limited because their range was self-limited to their own ranges of items. This meant buyers would buy the high value items from one store then need to go to the other store to pick up the impulse purchases – a transactional oxymoron!

Another issue with this disintermediation strategy was that it offended the toy stores that had previously been extremely loyal customers. They then sought out different suppliers of the same items.

In summary the strategy of disintermediation failed because the distributor had failed to recognise the value added by its distribution chain and the unique nature of the purchasing process for their products.

8.4 Free, premium and freemium e-distribution

One of the major developments resulting from the internet and on-line systems has been the rise of free services. Now virtually any service can be found on-line for free from email (starting with Hotmail and Google mail) to virus scanning (Avast and AVG), and a vast array of free software that can be downloaded from mobile phone games, web browsers, office software to Operating Systems. Being free there is little firm information on the size of the free download market but there have been over 20 million downloads of Ubuntu, 92 million downloads of Open Office (a free office competitor to MS Office) and over 1 billion downloads of the Angry Birds series of games. This demonstrates that the market for free software and services is huge.

Of course software and on-line services cost money to develop and provide and so, on the face of it, it is hard to understand the business model that supports such free software and services. If no-one is paying how can they be earning? The simple answer is in most cases Premium Services or versions which do cost money.

Each of the major software applications or on-line services has a free service offering which is usually limited to personal, non-commercial use and may have a restricted feature set (up-load/download limits, file size limits etc.). This is typical of services such as dropbox, Gmail etc.

In order to use the software or service commercially a fee is charged. Fees may also be charged for support contracts (usually required within commercial settings) or for access to more frequent bug fixes/patches. For example Ubuntu (which produces a linux 'distribution') offers the basic software for free but then sells support contracts to businesses. These support contracts cover the organisation's costs allowing the software to be given to home users for free. Indeed by seeding the market with many users this has the benefit of enhancing the market share and demonstrating its value to the corporate market.

Within the market for smaller scale downloads (particularly phone apps) the free app may be supported by pop-up ads and a premium service charged which removes the ads. The classic examples of this are games such as Angry Birds. Other examples are games which offer a variety of free levels to 'hook' the user or require paid-for add-ons to allow the player to progress. Much controversy has been raised by these in-game top-ups with many parents finding children had spent many £100s on additional top-ups for the games. This demonstrates the power of the top-up market and also the risks associated with the simplified payment mechanisms employed within mobile phone stores such as iTunes and Google Playstore where payment card details are stored and do not need to be re-entered.

This combination of a basic free service with a premium paid for service is generically known as the freemium model. Suppliers calculate that the offering of a free service will initially generate a substantial user base and that some of that base can then be converted into paying customers. These freemium services are notable for a number of common features:

- **Scalability** – once the software or service is developed the marginal costs for each customer are negligible
- **Potential for large customer base** – if conversion rates are single digit percentages then a very large customer base is required to support it

In essence this approach takes into account the fact that for a new product launch 20–50% of the revenue from each product sale could be attributed to marketing. By giving the product away and using that as the primary marketing tool only a relatively low conversion rate from free to premium is required in order to become cost effective.

Free for life services

There are a number of on-line services that are 'Free for Life' i.e. have no charges and no 'premium' offering. Social Media sites are the principal examples, though services such as Yahoo and many news sites also exist as 'free for life'. In essence these make most income from advertising, or in the case of ad-free services such as Twitter, from paid inclusions/promotions and/or offering for sale customer information or intelligence.

The widely known but unattributed quote "If you're not paying for it, you're not the customer, you're the product." implies that the supplier of the service is gaining from your participation in the service usually by gathering and reselling information.

Many Social Media (SM) sites harvest information either explicitly or implicitly though behavioural analysis (RT.com, 2013) to be able to fine tune advertisements to increase the click-through rate (CTR) and value per click. The more frequently a user interacts on a Social Media site then the more granular the profile becomes and so its value increases. Stock Market valuation of SM sites is greatly affected by the level and intensity of interaction of its active users. Within marketing it is now possible to fine tune campaigns through SM sites to maximise both CTR and the Conversion Rate.

Summary

In summary the core message from understanding distribution and the many different distribution models used is the need to understand the business value chain. Each element in the distribution chain adds unique value to the product or service offered and the determination of the summation of this value is crucial to understanding the business model used.

Within the marketing sphere, distribution incurs separation between the core of the business and the end user and, in the case of a complex value chain, can involve the preparation of different sets of marketing messages, different values and activities to each of the elements.

In an extended value chain the different motivations of the various stages must be taken into account. In many cases the overall strategy of the external elements may not align with that of the principal company and/or the end user and so careful management of these often conflicting aims is required.

Equally your brand and the values you associate with your brand may be conflicted when operating through a channel and so strong policies and procedures may be required in order to protect the values (and value) associated with the brand. This is of particular importance in the on-line marketplace where entry barriers are lower and it can be harder to maintain and control brand values.

In order to be an effective marketing professional, it is essential to understand how the business operates and how the different operating modes will affect how marketing can occur, and how best to control the overall marketing strategy and message.

References

Dedrick, J, Kraemer, K L and Linden, G (2010) *The Distribution of Value in the Mobile Phone Supply Chain*, [online], http://pcic.merage.uci.edu/papers/2010/CellPhoneProfitability_Oct2010.pdf (Accessed 25/06/2013)

Encana (2012) *Encana 1Q Profits Increase on Hedging Gains*, Rigzone, [online] http://www.rigzone.com/news/article.asp?a_id=117318 (Accessed 19/06/2013)

Hennart, J F (2010) Transaction Cost Theory and International Business, *Journal of Retailing*, Volume 86, Issue 3, September

House of Commons Treasury Committee (2011) *Competition and choice in retail banking*, [online], http://www.publications.parliament.uk/pa/cm201011/cmselect/cmtreasy/612/612i.pdf (Accessed 19/06/2013)

NetImperative (2011) *Top 50 online retailers in the UK*, NetImperative, [online], http://www.digitalstrategyconsulting.com/netimperative/news/2011/05/top_100_online_retailers_in_th.php (Accessed 19/06/2013)

Onlyinsurance.com, (n.d) *Car Insurance - More people switching car insurance providers than ever*, [online], http://www.onlyinsurance.com/Car-Insurance/More-people-switching-car-insurance-providers-than-ever.aspx (Accessed 19/06/2013)

ONS (2012) *Consumer Trends, Q3 2012*, [online], http://www.ons.gov.uk/ons/dcp171778_292282.pdf (Accessed 25/06/2013)

Poeter, D (2012) *The Strange, Campy Tale of the Web's Very First Photo*, PCMag, [online], http://www.pcmag.com/article2/0,2817,2407009,00.asp (Accessed 19/06/2013)

Porter, M E (2008) *On Competition*, Harvard Business Press Books

Publishing Perspectives (2012) *Looking at US E-book Statistics and Trends*, [online], http://publishingperspectives.com/2012/10/looking-at-us-e-book-statistics-and-trends/ (Accessed 25/06/2013)

Reilly, G (2012) *Over 1 billion apps downloaded in Christmas week*, [online], http://businessetc.thejournal.ie/over-1-billion-apps-downloaded-in-christmas-week-319441-Jan2012/ (Accessed 25/06/2013)

RT.com (2013) *Facebook knows your secrets: 'Likes' reveal users' personality*, RT.com, [online], http://rt.com/news/facebook-like-personality-study-139/ (Accessed 19/06/2013)

Segall, L (2012) *Facebook's stock dive is 'disappointing,' CEO Mark Zuckerberg says*, CNNMoney, [online], http://money.cnn.com/2012/09/11/technology/zuckerberg-techcrunch-disrupt/index.html (Accessed 19/06/2013)

Skrill (2011) *Online shopping returns 'cost fashion retailers £100 million a year'*, Skrill, [online], http://corporate.skrill.com/2011/07/online-shopping-returns-cost-fashion-retailers-100-million-a-year/2203/
(Accessed 19/06/2013)

Smith, D (2012) *Over 14 million UK current account holders may switch bank accounts under Vickers reforms*, SAS, [online], http://www.sas.com/offices/europe/uk/press_office/press_releases/UK-retail-banks-account-switching.html (Accessed 19/06/2013)

Sterling,G (2013) *Report: Nearly 40 Percent Of Internet Time Now On Mobile Devices*, Marketing Land, [online], http://marketingland.com/report-nearly-40-percent-of-internet-time-now-on-mobile-devices-34639 (Accessed 19/06/2013)

Wood, C (2007) *Compare and contrast: How the UK comparison website market is serving financial consumers*, Resolution Foundation, [online], http://www.resolutionfoundation.org/media/media/downloads/research_report_web comparison.pdf (Accessed 19/06/2013)

Wynne, A (2012) *Atkins drawn into dispute over Cambridgeshire guided busway*, NCE, [online], http://www.nce.co.uk/news/transport/atkins-drawn-into-dispute-over-cambridgeshire-guided-busway/8629750.article (Accessed 19/06/2013)

Index